FRANCHISING
HOW BOTH SIDES CAN WIN

CHRIS EDGER AND ANDREW EMMERSON

LIBRI
PUBLISHING

First published in 2015 by Libri Publishing

Copyright © Libri Publishing

ISBN 978-1-909818-60-6

A CIP catalogue record for this book is available from The British Library

Design by Carnegie Publishing

Cover design by Helen Taylor

Printed in the UK by Berforts Information Press

Libri Publishing
Brunel House
Volunteer Way
Faringdon
Oxfordshire
SN7 7YR

Tel: +44 (0)845 873 3837

www.libripublishing.co.uk

CONTENTS

SECTION 1 – HOW FRANCHISORS WIN

SECTION 2 – HOW FRANCHISEES WIN

LIST OF FIGURES

LIST OF ABBREVIATIONS

AVD – Added Value Deviance
BAU – Business as Usual
BCU – Birmingham City University
BFA – British Franchise Association
BOH – Back of House
BSE – Brand Service Experience
CEO – Chief Executive Officer
COG – Cost of Goods
COO – Chief Operating Officer
CSF – Critical Success Factors
CSI – Customer Service Index
DMA – District Marketing Association
DPG – Domino's Pizza Group
EBITDA – Earnings Before Interest, Taxation, Depreciation and Amortisation
EI – Emotional Intelligence
EMEA – Europe, Middle East and Asia
EPOS – Electronic Point of Sale
EQ – Emotional Quotient
FA – Franchise Agreement
FAQ – Frequently Asked Question
FCS – Franchise Control Systems
FDD – Full Disclosure Document
FEM – Franchise Exchange Model
FLIC – Franchisee Leadership Council
FOH – Front of House
FSM – Franchise Support Manager
GDP – Gross Domestic Product
GM – General Manager
HND – Higher National Diploma
HQ – Headquarters
HRM – Human Resource Management
IMF – International Master Franchisee
IP – Intellectual Property

IQ – Intellectual Quotient
IT – Information Technology
KFC – Kentucky Fried Chicken
KPI – Key Performance Indicator
MAC – Marketing Advisory Council
MCS – Management Control System
MD – Managing Director
MF – Master Franchisee
MMU – Mastering Multi-Units
MUF – Multiple Unit Franchisee
NWH – New World Hotels
OER – Operational Evaluation Review
OM – Operations Manual
OPI – Operational and Process Improvement
P&L – Profit and Loss
PR – Public Relations
ROI – Return on Investment
RTD – Regional Training Directors
SET – Social Exchange Theory
SSP – Select Service Partners
SUF – Single Unit Franchisee
SVP – Senior Vice President
SWOT – Strengths, Weaknesses, Opportunities, Threats
UK – United Kingdom
US – United States
USA – United States of America
VP – Vice President
YHA – Youth Hostel Association

ABOUT THE AUTHORS

Professor Chris Edger is the author of *Effective Multi-Unit Leadership* (described by the *Leadership and Organization Development Journal* as 'one of the key books of its kind for this decade'), *International Multi-Unit Leadership*, *Professional Area Management* and *Area Management – Strategic and Local Models for Organic Growth* (forthcoming, 2016). Frequently called upon to commentate upon retail issues within the UK media, Chris has been described as 'the UK's leading expert on multi-site management'. He is also the Founder Director of the Multi-Unit Leadership and Strategy Programme at Birmingham City University, UK that specialises in training and developing retail multi-site managers. Prior to academia, Chris held executive director positions in UK, US and European owned multi-unit enterprises. During the course of his career he was Commercial Development Director for a leisure firm that held the master franchise for the roll-out of two US brands in the UK. He holds a PhD (ESRC Award, Warwick Business School) and an MSc (econ) with distinction (London School of Economics).

Andrew Emmerson is the owner of the Emmerson Development Company which advises SMEs and large companies on franchising. Until 2014 he was UK Executive Director of Franchising and Development for Domino's Pizza, having previously held senior executive positions leading/developing/rolling-out Millie's Cookies (UK), Upper Crust (Europe) and Dunkin' Donuts (US). Andrew is currently non-executive chairman of the Snappy Snaps chain, a non-executive at Hotcha and The Victorian Chop House Company, and co-owns three Dunkin' Donuts franchises in the US. Andrew holds an LLB Hons (University of Liverpool).

ACKNOWLEDGEMENTS

This book has benefited from the contributions, insights and advice of many people over the last couple of years; not least Paul Charity (Founder, Propelinfo), Professor Duncan Angwin (Oxford Brookes), David Evans QC, Paul Jervis (publisher, Libri), Professor Gerald Noone OBE (Newcastle), Dr Clinton Bantock (BCU) and Stephen Willson (BCU).

The authors would especially like to thank the interviewees and contributors to this book, who were (in case-study order): Chris Moore (ex-CEO Domino's), Misha Zelman (co-founder Burger and Lobster), John Pratt (Hamilton Pratt), Maurice Abboudi (founder Famous Moe's Pizza and K10), Paul Daynes (ex-L&D Executive, Musgraves), Bryn Thomas (Finance Director, Citroen UK), Jerry Robinson (National Operations Director, Youth Hostel Association), Patricia Thomas (ex-Operations and International Director, Domino's), Andrew Thomas (Operations Director, Dome Café, Australia), Clive Chesser (ex-Operations Director, Häagen-Dazs International), Jerry Marwood (MD, Blakemore Spar Trade Partners), Adrian Rhodes (ARConsulting, GlobalBrand), Richard Johnson (Multiple Franchisee, Domino's), John Brighthouse (Single Unit Franchisee, Glasses Inc), Lee Sheldon (ex-Global Learning and Development Director SSP), Ian Dunstall (ex-SVP Marketing, Rosinter Restaurants, Russia), Alex Dawson (ex-Operations Director, Café2U) and Kelly-Ann Grimes (Operations Director, New World Hotels). Thank you all for reviewing various sections of the book and your outstanding case-study contributions.

Chris would (again) like to thank his wife Sheenagh for her support and understanding during his research and back-to-back authorship of a five-book series on multi-site retail businesses. Andrew would like to thank his wife Jackie for her fantastic backing during this book and his long commercial career – he has no further plans to take on more business interests (but he has had a few more offers… !)

CHAPTER 1
INTRODUCTION

Retail format franchising is an inter-company transaction that involves one party (the franchisor) licensing to another party (the franchisee) singular and/or multiple rights to copy a unique retail, leisure or service business model that profitably addresses a viable customer segment. For franchisors, it is a low-risk form of expansion in which capital, liabilities and responsibilities are shared through the co-option of a network of highly incentivised and motivated franchisees. For franchisees, the benefits of such an arrangement stem from the fact that they are limiting their business risk through buying into a legally regulated form of industrial systemisation which promises all the benefits of scale, brand identification/reputation and business acumen. Its business antecedents lie in eighteenth-century merchant licensing, but more latterly – since the depression-riven 1930s in the USA – as a vehicle for rapid chain growth. Today, with increasing customer mobility (both physically and digitally), franchised formats which promise quality and consistency remain highly popular with customers and are of huge significance to developed-/growth-market service-sector GDPs. In the UK for instance, franchising grew 20% during 2008–2012 (compared to a 2.5% contraction in the economy over the same period) with the sector contributing £14bn to GDP and providing 560,000 jobs in 2013 (NatWest/BFA 2013).

Clearly, this is a vital and vibrant form of business arrangement but its success relies on a critical interdependence between two parties – the franchisor and franchisee – neither of whom can succeed without the other. But what are the activities and critical success factors for both these parties? How do both parties win? To this extent, this book will build upon previous 'how to' franchising guides and academic commentaries by offering a framework – based on previous literature, the authors' own commercial knowledge and research – of how both parties can succeed 'mutually'. In particular, how both sides (i.e. both franchisor and franchisee) can win will be illuminated by isolating the base qualifiers and differentiators for success. Additionally, this book is anchored by nineteen major retail-related case studies that will provide voices and vibrancy to reinforce the text – something that should be a major attraction both to practitioners and to students operating within this area.

The main theme running through this book (which is based on empirical research and grounded experience/observation) will be that the universal explanation for successful relations between business parties is not purely one of agency – where the principal (franchisor) provides economic incentives and monitors their agents (franchisee) for assured behaviours/financial outcomes. In this, our argument is contrary to most texts relating to franchising. Rather, it suggests that social exchange provides a far more compelling guiding explanation of how both sides win. According to Social Exchange Theory (SET), parties with a high level of mutual interdependence are governed by the laws of reciprocity and indebtedness. Alignment, good relations and high levels of satisfaction are achieved through the fair and trusting exchange of love, money, status, information, products and services (Foa and Foa 1974, 1980). Therefore, a contribution of this book will be its central theme of exchange rather than agency as the principal cause of both sides winning within franchising.

But what does the existing research and literature say about the success factors relating to both parties in the retail franchising arrangement? An understanding of what has already been established is essential to understand gaps and avenues for further commentary.

PRIOR LITERATURE AND RESEARCH

Over the past fifty years, franchising has been examined from two principal dimensions: practitioner and academic. The practitioner literature has spawned two types of genre – 'How I did it' accounts and 'How to do it' guides. The former, exemplified by books such as the seminal *Grinding It Out* by Ray Kroc (1977), provide plenty of pithy insights into the 'dos' and 'don'ts' of franchising from both franchisor and franchisee perspectives. In this excerpt, Ray Kroc explains the thinking that lay behind franchising the brand (uniformity and quality) and his means of differentiating the concept from competitors (forming a quasi-property company that developed the best sites):

We agreed that we wanted McDonald's to be more than just a name used by many different people. We wanted to build a restaurant system that would be known for food of consistently high quality and uniform methods of preparation. Our aim, of course, was to insure [sic] repeat business based on the system's reputation rather than on a single store or operator. This would require a continuing program of educating and assisting operators and a constant review of their performance [and] our ability to provide techniques of preparation that operators would accept because they were superior to methods they could dream up themselves… [Also we concluded] that the only practical way for McDonald's to grow as we envisioned would be for us to develop the restaurants ourselves. Being in the restaurant [real estate] development business would mean that we could plan a strong system in which locations could be developed by McDonald's… [making] the right to operate a McDonald's restaurant far more valuable to a potential operator than if we were franchising only a name…

(Kroc, 1977: 86–7)

Of course, the story of McDonald's – the reasons behind its growth and sustained success – provides many lessons on 'how to' build and (from the franchisee's perspective) choose a great franchised business format chain, something that a plethora of books have sought to describe and illuminate (see Gibson 2010, Duckett and Monaghan 2007, Spinelli et al. 2004, Mendelsohn 1999). Many of these books have words such as 'grow', 'success' and 'wealth creation' in their sub-titles and give detailed step-by-step advice to would-be franchisors and franchisees on 'how to' make the right sequence of decisions and choices in their putative franchising journeys. However, these excellent guides generally suffer from a lack of an isolation of the key differentiators (as opposed to hygiene factors) that might lead to greater effectiveness; insufficient 'real voices' or case studies that bring alive their extensive check lists; and a general propensity to describe success factors relating to one party (i.e. franchisor) rather than a consideration of the winning attributes of both sides.

Something which is also ignored or dismissed by the practitioner literature is the voluminous academic commentary on franchising. This is an important omission. Over the past forty years academics have researched the franchised domain, utilising a number of theoretical lenses and perspectives to understand origins/patterns of success and/or failure. Broadly, this literature can be sub-divided into three distinct genres: **transactional** (including economic and legal perspectives), **relational** (psychological and sociological perspectives) and **developmental** (strategic, marketing and international perspectives). The first stream of research locates itself in a paradigm that views the success of the relationship between the franchisor and franchisee as being based around a series of discreet contractual and economic interactions, with **high-quality transactions** (centered around fairness and equity) leading to favourable outcomes for both parties. The second literature sees success as being based around **high-quality relations** which sustain commitment and satisfaction levels even when there are transactional problems between the two parties. The last commentary locates franchising success as lying in **developmental capability**; resource-based strategies of the firm, category/channel/distribution targeting and international paths providing explanations for growth and expansion. But how does the research within these three broad approaches inform us about the reasons for success/failure in franchising?

TRANSACTIONAL EXPLANATIONS

Economic perspective – This view uses **agency theory** (Jensen and Meckling 1976, Eisenhardt 1989) as a universal explanation for franchising success/failure. In franchising, the principal (franchisor) can control its agent (franchisee) through **incentives** (a profitable systemised format that reduces franchisee **search costs**) thereby reducing its own **monitoring costs** (i.e. costs of directly supervising unit operations). Unlike managers in company-owned stores, franchisees have incentives to perform and exert more effort due to costs relating to breaches/non-compliance (financial sanctions or termination) that threaten their personal wealth or security. The monitoring costs of the franchisor hypothetically are low because of these incentives *although* costs can arise through the **moral hazard** (sub-optimal effort) posed by **adverse selection** (poor recruitment decisions), **free-riding** (when the franchisee draws down value from the brand – reputation and services – without reciprocating) and **shirking** (when franchisees degrade the wider network by avoiding responsibilities such as operating manual adherence). Significant research suggests that this form of **opportunism** arises less in multiple (MUF) rather than single (SUF) unit franchise contexts because of higher incentives to **bond** and lack of **resource scarcity** (capital and people) improving uniformity, monitoring, knowledge transfer and innovation capabilities (Lafontaine 1992, Klein 1995, Weaven and Frazer 2007a).

Legal perspective – In essence the 'franchise relationship is an intermediate between a single firm and a market **transaction**' (Rubin 1978: 232).

This means that there is an inter-firm contractual relationship that confers a myriad of duties and obligations on both parties. The legal view examines the liabilities and rights of both parties from both a **regulatory** and **contractual** standpoint (Gellhorn 1967, Pfister et al. 2006). From a regulatory perspective, academics have noted how government agencies have increasingly sought to promote fairness and transparency in the relationship by imposing rules relating to **pre-contractual disclosure** (to prevent **information asymmetry** between the partners) and **anti-encroachment legislation** to protect franchisee territories. In addition, academics have tracked mounting liabilities for franchisors as contract law builds within this area, especially with regard to matters such as: **direct franchisor negligence**, **vicarious liability**, **strict product liability**, **negligent representation** and **breach of warranties of fitness**. Some of these liabilities can be mitigated by the way in which franchisors design their contracts, systems and franchise operations manuals, pre-empting the manner in which courts might interpret relations/transactions as being 'independent' or 'master–servant'. From a franchisee perspective, academics have documented how certain disadvantages might flow from the franchising contract, not least the fact that having to follow strictly certain policies, measures and practices can attract onerous penalties (termination or non-renewal) stifling innovation and local flexibility (Pfister et al. 2006).

RELATIONAL EXPLANATIONS

Psychological perspective – In this domain academics have located franchising success through constructs such as **commitment** and **satisfaction**. To these commentators, transactional explanations are insufficient. There are bound to be road-bumps in the commercial relationship – so how are these issues ameliorated/overcome and why? For relational theorists the answer lies in constructs such as a positive '**psychological climate**' (Strutton et al. 1995). Good long-term relations are sustained where perceptions of 'justice, cohesion, innovation and autonomy' prevail. However, '**psychological attachment**' between the partners begins at the contractual stage where franchisees form realistic **expectations** of what the franchisor is offering, which is then matched or exceeded by the levels of 'open communication, **perceived support** and levels of individual decision-making' that are afforded 'in flight' (Grace et al. 2013):

> franchisors need to remain cognizant that the key to fostering mutually beneficial franchising relationships lies in understanding the

composition of a franchisee's initial expectations associated with franchising as a business model. Indeed the (dis)confirmation of these expectations play a pivotal role in framing perceptions of franchisor-provided services, significantly reduce franchisee's perceptions of conflict within the system and significantly enhance relationship satisfaction...

(Grace et al. 2013: 228)

When correctly **profiled** franchisees with right **personalites** (aspirational, agreeable and conscientious) have entered the system, maintaining **goal alignment/job satisfaction** through the **franchisee 'lifecycle'** is contingent on maintaining high levels of support (operations, business, product and marketing) which (hypothetically) has four organisational outcomes: performance, organisational commitment, franchisor relations and intentions to remain (Morrison 1997, Dant et al. 2013). In addition, costs for the franchisor are reduced by the reduction of opportunistic behaviours and the need to deploy controls and safeguards. In fact, good relations within the network can be viewed as an **intrinsic source of value** for the franchisor, given that many chains are more interested in investing in tangible assets (site, layout, machines and technology) rather than intangible assets such as the franchisor–franchisee relationship where it is more difficult to establish an ROI (Madhok and Tallman 1998).

Sociological perspective – To sociologists, relationships within organisations are not shaped by individual psychological dispositions; rather they are mediated by structures/cultures in which actors, through their **power resources**, can either create cupertino relationships or **conflict** (Palamountain 1955). Franchisors have three sources of power: **persuasion** through communications, franchisee support as a means of **exchange** or **coercive power** to manipulate franchisee actions (Hunt and Nevin 1974). Indeed, the type of power that is wielded is argued to have an effect on franchisee satisfaction and results: '**economic**' coercive/legitimate power and '**non-economic**' referent/information power sources having, respectively, negative and positive outcomes (Parsa 1996). The literature in this area suggests that successful franchisors apply 'economic' power appropriately, focusing on building long-term relationships through adopting **flexible control approaches** (i.e. Spinelli et al.'s 2004 'zone of tolerance') and high levels of **reciprocity-based behaviour** into the relationship (Kaufmann and Dant 1992, Diaz-Bernardo 2013). Conflict is reduced if franchisees form part of their network's **decision-making structure** (through local/regional/national meetings and associations) and – most importantly

– franchisors restrain their urge to abuse their economic sources of power by '**gorging**'; driving sales to maximise royalties rather than optimising franchisee margin/profit growth (Spinelli and Birley 1998).

DEVELOPMENTAL EXPLANATIONS

Strategic perspective – Commentators operating within this paradigm argue that success is also dependent on franchisors adopting an '**executive leadership**' style, nurturing **inimitable resources/agility** through appropriate **organisational design** and an effective **learning culture**. Researchers argue that in spite of the need to encourage franchisees to contribute to the decision-making process, an '**executive**' (inspiring and directing) rather than exclusively '**participative**' (involving and empowering) leadership style is more appropriate when it comes to reducing conflict and increasing co-operation (Schul et al. 1983). It is particularly important as the franchisor transitions through organisational configurations (Castrogiovanni and Justis 1998): **entrepreneurial** (inception), **confederation** (loosely coupled due to heterogenous/unstable markets) or **carbon-copy** (tightly bound through facing homogeneous/stable markets) and back to **entrepreneurial** (when a turnaround requires strong and decisive leadership). Effective leaders also take a '**resource-based view**' of the firm, where they invest in strategic capabilities (infrastructure, training and services), growing 'absorptive capacity' by encouraging inimitable/tacit knowledge to develop within an '**organisational learning context**' (Sorenson and Sorenson 2001, DiPietro et al. 2008, Weaven and Frazer 2007b, Michael and Combs 2008). To this end, researchers argue, franchisors are well advised to devise a 20/80 split in their estate between company-owned stores and franchises because franchised stores provide better opportunities (due to entrepreneurial risk-taking/autonomous mindsets) for firms to learn through experimentation whilst the company-owned ones facilitate a better means of rolling-out and standardising change.

Marketing perspective – Academics working from this perspective regard franchising success as being highly connected to **category positioning**, **market insight** and effective **channel/distribution** construction. With regards to categories, it is highly desirable for start-up franchisors to be positioned within **growth segments** – current examples from a *business format* standpoint in developed contexts including: food service/restaurants, children's/students' educational services and elderly care provision (Anwar 2011). Within identified growth categories franchisors should take care to build differentiated quality/value '**service delivery systems**' (Spinelli et al. 2004) whilst establishing strong networks. Site selection is key to network strength, a process aided by developments in the field of '**psychographics**' (as opposed to traditional demographic insight) which concentrates upon identifying 'hotspots' through analysing **customer** lifestyles and buying habits by aggregating and analysing multiple pools of data (Hollander 2005). More often than not, effective networks are built through offering **exclusive territories**; high levels of franchisee performance being more guaranteed by ensuring that they feel protected – more able to benefit from their localised efforts. This success factor is endorsed by several studies which have empirically demonstrated 'same brand franchisee encroachers' are more impactful upon revenues than competitors (Kalnins 2004). This territorial saliency within networks also induces the fostering of '**strong vertical/horizontal ties**' between both the main parties and amongst the franchisees' multiple units.

International perspective – A large academic literature examining franchising as a route to international expansion points to three main drivers of success which are related to **institutional, cultural** and **strategic** factors (Doherty 2007, Baena 2012, Edger 2013). From an **institutional** point of view, **national business systems** (NBS) charateristics – especially in developing markets – are important. Expanding organisations are more likely to be successful in developing NBSs that have a high level of economic potential (accompanied by low levels of inflation and stable exchange rates), low levels of corruption, moderate competitive intensity (a fragmented 'independent' sector being highly desirable) and sound rules of law/legal protection (particularly those relating to trademarks and employment). From a **cultural** perspective many developing markets will display challenging characteristics (as defined by Hofstede 1991) that can pose problems for Western styles of management, including: **high-power distance/masculinity** (propensity for self-protective leadership behaviour), **high uncertainty avoidance** (people want to be told what to do to avoid accountability/responsibility due to potential failure and a 'fear of retribution'), **high levels of in-group collectivism** (a 'village type' mentality that is suspicious of outsiders) and **low levels of achievement orientation** (where relationships/nepotism are valued more highly than business outcomes). Added to this, cultural differences will ensure that idiosyncratic tastes, preferences and nuances will vary in any given market. Understanding and addressing many of these issues is difficult given problems of **geographical/'psychic' distance**, and so (unsurprisingly) the most prevalent **strategic mode of entry** into new developing markets is the **Master Franchising** (MF) route. In this arrangement, 'home franchisors' select a local partner as a licensed partner to roll-out their concept themselves and/or by recruiting local franchisees. Failure between the two parties usually occurs through factors such as lack of mutual understanding, low trust caused by information asymmetry, poor commitment/unreliability, divergence of professional/educational back-grounds and cultural incompatibilities. Franchisors stand a higher chance of success with their MFs if they possess previous franchise experience, sufficient capital and excellent local knowledge (particularly with regards to site finding, product demand and marketing channels). The first factor is important – co-opting an MF that already runs other franchised concepts grants more of a chance of success given their prior experience in 'trans-lating' concepts and working with foreign partners but also because they can make substantial savings through common back offices and sharing employees across brands (Alon 2006).

But what are we to make of all this research; what are its contributions and gaps? The first (and obvious!) thing to say is that franchising has been examined empirically from a number of dimensions, substantially increasing our understanding of critical success factors for both parties. Transactional ('economic'), relational ('non-economic') and development/strategic perspectives greatly assist our understanding of how both sides can win. What is lacking however (in spite of the 'how I did it' texts referred to above) are **case-study-based voices** that will add colour to the largely survey-based academic literature and 'how to' lists of eponymous fran-chising guides. In addition, clarity is required to locate not just the **base qualifiers** for success but – more importantly – **differentiators** that give clarity to professionals as to the *key* ingredients for success. Based on previous investigations, the practice-based experience of the authors and contemporary research, these are gaps that this book will attempt to fill.

STRUCTURE AND CONTENT OF THE BOOK

In order to address the key question posed by this book – how can both parties (franchisor and franchisee) win in a retail franchising context – the book is divided into two parts, one addressing franchisor and the other exploring franchisee **activities** and critical success factors (CSFs). Further-more, the book is designed around a guiding conceptual framework that highlights key areas for both parties (see Figure 1 below). Thus, chap-ters 2 to 4 will examine how franchisors successfully **design**, **deliver** and

develop their franchised business formats. This is followed from chapters 5 to 7 by how franchisees effectively **engage**, **execute** and **evolve** during their franchising journey. Sub-components of each area will explore, in depth, the base qualifiers and differentiators for success backed up by illustrative 'real-life' case studies from both parties.

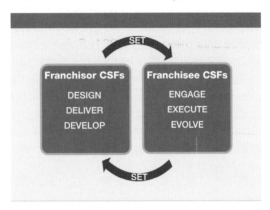

Figure 1.1: Franchising Critical Success Factor Framework

One important component of the conceptual framework outlined above is the pictorial representation (through the arched arrows) of the symbiosis between both parties. This mutuality is a theme that runs consistently through this book, leading to an underlying theoretical explanation for franchising success for both partners – namely, social exchange theory (SET). This theoretical perspective advances the notion that organisations can only achieve sustainable performance through trust-based socio-emotional transactions with followers/partners, where perceived benefits outweigh costs (Cropanzano and Mitchell 2005, Saks 2006):

> Social exchange theory (SET) argues that obligations are generated through a series of interactions between parties who are in a state of reciprocal interdependence. A basic tenet of SET is that relationships evolve over time into trusting, loyal, and mutual commitments as long as the parties abide by certain 'rules' of exchange (Cropanzano and Mitchell, 2005). Rules of exchange usually involve reciprocity or repayment rules such that the actions of one party lead to a response or actions by the other party...

> (Saks 2006: 603)

Thus, social exchange theory conceives of business relations being governed by the law of reciprocity where a general social *indebtedness* is shaped, forming the basis of a community that can be kept in balance over time and across teams/parties (Meeker 1971, Emerson 1976). There are six archetypes of exchange, including: love, money, status, information, goods and services (Foa and Foa 1974, 1980). Exchanges are governed by the laws of reciprocity in which clear mutual gains are made by each party through transmission mechanisms such as mutual goal attainment, free market exchange, compensated costs and the uncovering of hidden value (Gouldner 1960, Blau 1964, Cohen and Bradford 1989). The **summaries** of each chapter will highlight the importance of social exchange as a 'binding' factor in franchisor–franchisee relations, which is a critical component of enabling both sides to win. The major contribution of this book – a **Franchise Exchange Model** (FEM) which provides a universal explanation of successful mutuality between the two parties – is outlined in the **conclusion**.

This book will look next at franchisor *activities* and critical success factors. However, before it does, it will be useful to introduce the first 'voice' to this book who – in order to provide context – gives his expert view (based on his own significant commercial experience building one of the UK's most valuable franchised organisations) on how both parties can win in franchising.

Case Study 1 – Give and Take – How Both Sides Can Win

Chris Moore spent 22 years with Domino's Pizza, firstly with the US and European operations, subsequently playing a major part in the team that set up the UK Master Franchise in 1993. During his time at Domino's Pizza Group (DPG) UK – where he eventually became COO and then CEO – Chris assisted its stellar growth from 37 to over 700 stores, establishing DPG as one of the most successful and valuable franchised networks in the UK. Prior to Domino's, Chris was an account director at McCann Erikson; he is now a serial business investor and international consultant in franchising.

It's easy for companies to say 'let's franchise!' only thinking about the financial upside and how they can grow a brand using other

CONTINUED ...

people's capital... but I have always believed that you can only build a successful and sustainable franchised business by adopting a *'win–win'* mentality which builds trusting, long-term relationships... So how do both sides win? ...

Franchisors will win if they understand that, firstly, it is more about the *EQ (emotional intelligence)* than the IQ... secondly, it is about establishing hard 'number-grinding' *financial advantages*... Let me illustrate these points by highlighting what we did at DPG:

- **Emotional Intelligence**... when I say that successful franchisors win by having a good EQ what I mean is they attend to the (more difficult) *'softer', cultural* side of the organisation in order to achieve 'hard' tangible outcomes... What we did at DPG was to produce a culture that was *'akin to a club'* where we could persuade and coerce members to do the 'right thing' for the greater good. The way in which we did this was:

  - *Stick to a Mission*... people at all levels of the organisation needed to know what we were all about... our Company mantra was 'Sell More Pizza, Have More Fun'... simple, quirky, engaging, resonant...

  - *Leadership Stability*... building up the network, we were signing up franchisees for long periods of time... it was important (doubly so when we abandoned owned stores) to have knowledgeable, credible leaders... with high levels of operational/support expertise and strong franchisee ties... You have to have a system based on long-term relationships... The fact that at one time our leadership team had an average of 13 years' service was incredibly important for information/knowledge continuity purposes...

  - *Communication & Recognition*... at DPG, in addition to district and regional meetings, we held two major set-piece events which were *deliberately inclusive*... In October every year we had a managers' conference where we 'got them pumped up' for Xmas... Our key event was the DPG awards ceremony in March/April where, after having business and information sessions at the beginning we had a 'big bash' at the end... But the point is this: we didn't only invite franchisees, we also

CONTINUED ...

invited their partners (who bear as much, if not more, of the burden!) and franchisees invited managers, along with other staff members and drivers that had been nominated for the top awards... the mood and spirit was phenomenal – it really *'glued us together'* for the year... even some of the franchisees and leadership team joined me in getting dressed up on stage (I made a great Marilyn Monroe and a cracking Queen!) and we made fun of ourselves... We chanted *'Who Are We: Domino's!, What Are We: Number One!, What Do We Do? – Sell More Pizzas, Have More Fun!!!'* ... This 'anglicised Americanism', as I call it, might seem trite to cynics – but it worked – for a few days we were all together... bonding... celebrating winning... with precious little sense of hierarchy and looking forward to winning together over the next year! ...

- **Financial Advantage**
  - *Equitable Share...* the way in which you 'divide up the profit pig' is also critical... to my mind a proper share that worked for DPG (as a quoted company) was 1/3 (franchisor), 2/3 (franchisee)... when things were challenging – particularly during food-cost inflation spurts and the subsequent credit crunch in the late noughties – we tried to keep to this split by maintaining product cash profit (at the expense of erosions in net margin...)
  - *Growth Opportunities...* we also rewarded the best by offering them store growth opportunities... At one point, we had too few stores per franchisee (2.7 in 2005) – making the network expensive/hard to monitor, with some poor-quality operators 'squatting' in large territories... as store valuations were linked to an ever-increasing multiple of sales, franchisees that were less engaged with the 'club' and the brand were tempted to sell up by increasingly attractive exit values... At DPG, we had the ultimate control as to which franchisees could expand... this meant that – over time – the quality of the franchisees in the system improved substantially as the more mediocre operators were bought out by those franchisees that really understood the 'club rules'... so by re-engineering

CONTINUED ...

the network (buying and 'breaching' free-loaders out) we not only rewarded good operators by giving them more outlets (the ratio went up to 5 stores per franchisee by 2010), net sales per store also rose significantly (from £10k to £15k per store)... this was a real '*win–win*' for both parties! ...

If these are the major ways in which the franchisor can 'win', the franchisee can also contribute to the relationship... again I'll use DPG as the example:

- **Local Knowledge**... at DPG about 70% of the core menu was fixed with the 'classics', allowing considerable latitude for franchisees to cater for local tastes (with different toppings and sides)... pricing was set at a local level by the franchisee depending on demographics/disposable incomes... also franchisees had a lot of flexibility regarding local promotions... This meant that operators with good local knowledge could make a real impact in their proximal markets... great local knowledge enabled franchisees to win on the ground and (financially) benefit the wider system! ...

- **Personal Energy**... allied to this knowledge, however, great franchisees required extraordinary energy reserves... the service delivery system in DPG is slick because 'sales timeslots' are narrow... you have to organise, monitor, motivate and mobilise resources quickly and effectively in order to win! ... this takes passion, energy, belief and commitment to the cause... energising those around you to demonstrate the same behaviours! ...

- **Mature Participation**... at DPG we had advisory groups that coalesced around our four core processes: menu development, IT, marketing and operations... to be invited onto these groups was a privilege and we expected mature contributions from 'seasoned' people... all were treated respectfully as equal partners at these meetings; all views were counselled... The best franchisees who commented on 'contentious' issues such as the supply chain or cost of goods did so politely and *rationally*... DPG was really a club – and to be a member of that club, all participants (both franchisor and franchisee) had to abide by certain rules so that both sides could win through 'selling more pizzas, having more fun!' ...

Questions for Both Parties (that arise from the case study above)

1. **Franchisors**
   a. Relational – How effective is the 'cultural binding' of your organisation? How do you *recognise* the contribution of your franchisees? How *inclusive* are you? How do you communicate *honestly* with, and *listen* to, your franchisees?
   b. Transactional – How effective is your business model and/or financial arrangement with your franchisees? How are franchisees *incentivised* to drive sales and grow? Do you have a *quality* product backed up by excellent support *expertise*?

2. **Franchisees**
   a. Relational – What is your level of *commitment* to the brand? Do you have a *respectful* attitude to the franchisor? To what degree do you *share* insights and local knowledge with the franchisor and your peers?
   b. Transactional – Are you deploying maximum financial resources to *grow* your business(es)? Are you *complying* with the main tenets of the brand whilst *collaborating* with the franchisor on 'new ways' of doing things?

SECTION 1
HOW FRANCHISORS WIN

DESIGN

The Introduction outlined a conceptual model that acts as the integrating framework for this book. In essence, the model divides the essential activities of both franchisors and franchisees into three areas, which – in the case of the former – includes **design**, **delivery** and **develop**. Each of these areas has a set of sequential sub-components that are vital to the success of the franchisor. In the case of *design* – the first area of activity for franchisors – these sub-components include conceiving/shaping a *'big idea'*, building the main *cornerstones* of the concept and *network* development. Consideration of each of these elements will include definitions, common problems, base qualifiers and differentiators for success, followed by a contemporaneous case study that illuminates each critical factor.

'BIG IDEA'

Finding a 'market place with a market space' for a scalable franchised retail format is a non-trivial challenge. The origins of most franchised concepts stem from existing successful businesses (either managed corporates or independently run SMEs), 'greenfield' NPD or imported brands. Owner/inventors have typically resorted to franchising for a variety of reasons including:

- **Capital constraints** – franchisors can 'pass on' costs in stores, people, buying and distribution to franchisees to resolve 'access to capital' and risk issues.

- **'Spatial pre-emption'** – rapid expansion (using agency capital, resources and energy) to achieve first mover advantage in securing key sites/territorial primacy.

- **Superior control** – network resilience (standards, systems and service) is improved – compared with managed stores – through the franchisee 'incentive' to comply with the agreement and blueprint (the costs of non-compliance potentially resulting in severe penalties).

- **'Local acuity'** – the appointment of franchisees with high levels of local knowledge sharpens tailored marketing/promotions and staff recruitment.
- **'Managed ceiling'** – managed stores that are uneconomic to run directly (with associated infrastructure costs and high levels of 'shirking') might be more viable in highly incentivised franchise arrangements.

However, franchising is not a route that many service businesses should pursue; obvious reasons including the fact that they are either insufficiently differentiated, too complex for scalability and/or too profitable as managed concepts. So what are the *base qualifiers* for success? These can be broken down into three areas – positioning, trialling and collateral:

- **Positioning and business model**
  - *Distinctive* **–** the products and services provided by the concept should address a *serviceable market* with genuine *customer need* but must offer something different in terms of *quality*, *value* and/or *speed*. This can be derived from a totally *new format* or an '*innovative iteration*' on an existing concept (generated from facility, technology, machinery and/or materials/supply chain innovation).
  - *Accretive* **–** the format should yield sufficient cash margin (after total costs) to offer sufficient *incentives* to potential franchisees in terms of *net earnings* (equivalent to a salaried job) and *payback* (a return on initial investment within at least a three-to-five-year period). In addition, the concept must generate sufficient sales for the franchisor to capture sufficient royalty and 'tied product' revenue.
  - *Simple* **–** the concept must be simple to *operate* (in order to train franchisees), *standardise* (to control and monitor outputs) and *replicate* (to roll out quickly).
  - *Flexible* **–** sufficient flexibility should be built into the business model for the purposes of constant *invention* and *improvement* to keep ahead of imitators and nimble 'second movers'.
- **Trialling/Piloting**
  - *'Proof of concept'* **–** piloting the concept for at least a year

either directly by the owner or through a co-opted 'employee' or a 'reduced' fee franchisee is essential to prove its viability (in terms of sales, fixed/variable costs and net profit) for multiple stakeholders i.e. franchisor, potential franchisees, banks, investors etc.

- **Resilience** – trialling also affords the franchisor the opportunity to increase the resilience of the concept by improving product-/service-delivery systems and testing price elasticities (upwards rather than downwards!).

- **Collateral**
  - **Capital** – one of the main qualifiers of success for franchisees is sufficient funding for professional services (franchise consultants, lawyers and financial advisors) to assist in robustly constructing all aspect of the concept. Costs associated with *concept design/appraisal, strategic/ business planning, piloting, sales/marketing/advertising* and *support infrastructure* are often vastly underestimated by start-up franchises. Serious franchisors must build lines of credit (either through private resources, borrowing and/or equity investment) that provide 3–5 years of funding. McDonald's did not break even for Ray Kroc until its tenth year!
  - **IP** – the intellectual collateral (trademarks, logos and/or proprietorial systems) must be protected through legal registering. This is particularly important in the concept's domestic environment but franchisors should also consider protecting their IP in potential foreign markets.

Addressing the factors above (which are described in detail by many 'how to' books) will provide some assurance of success for prospective franchisors. But what are the 'big idea' *differentiators* that really set the winners apart?

- **Monetary return** – proper *incentives* and proven financial returns for all stakeholders are essential. The financial model must be stress-tested violently in multiple scenarios (actual and simulated) to address stakeholder 'what if' questions/concerns.

- **Purpose/Meaning** – all successful franchises have an explicit/ tacit purpose (the reason for existence, 'the why') that connects with all stakeholders (staff, franchisees, investors and customers). This 'true north' will enable the concept to maintain its coherence, *recognition* and momentum through good times and bad.

- **Inimitability/Sustainability** – products and services (the 'what' and 'how') should not only be clearly defined/specified but be hard to copy and have prospects for longevity within the marketplace.

Case Study 2 – The Monoproduct 'Big Idea'

Burger & Lobster is a successful monoproduct concept (favourably reviewed by some commentators as the best type of 'premium fast food') that, having launched to great acclaim in London in 2012, is now examining international franchise opportunities outside of its UK–US heartlands. In this mission statement, one of its founders – the brilliant cuisineur Misha Zelman – describes the 'big idea' underpinning the brand.

Monoproduct Manifesto

I believe that a restaurant with just one dish on the menu can be popular – and financially successful. Want to know why? Read on and comment on my Manifesto.

Monoproduct Philosophy

The concept of a monoproduct restaurant is a reflection of fairly common global processes on a particular market place, which are linked to many aspects of modern life. These processes are the result of rapidly developing technologies, which accelerate change and stimulate consumption. Manufacturers offer all they have and by so doing provoke in consumers a defensive reaction against the limitless choice and chaos produced by it. There is a need for a new service which can be called 'making choices for you'.

In medieval times, in so-called 'restaurants', there had never been a huge menu for quite objective reasons (primitive food technology): it simply could not have existed. Nowadays we consciously try to make menus less extensive. There is a theory that civilisation

CONTINUED ...

develops in cycles. In regard to consumption, we also are going back to where it had all started. Truly global craftsmen are appearing who offer a small choice of unique products – just one phone, one tablet, etc. After having opened my first monoproduct restaurant, 'Burger&Lobster' (*Yes, I know... TWO products!!*), in London at the beginning of this year, I've confirmed with my own experience: this trend is applicable on the global restaurant market as well.

Today globalisation, cosmopolitanism and tolerance are eroding national borders. This allows us, the Russians, to open steak houses in London and Zurich, where American meat is cooked in Spanish ovens – and to make them both popular and successful. I'm not saying I've invented the bicycle; no-one is saying that there have never been establishments similar to monoproduct restaurants before. There have always been pizzerias, dumpling-bars (*rus. Pelmennaya*) or chebureks-houses (Central Asian) but they all existed outside of the global competition that exists today and they force us to create a 'cult' of one dish and do our best to make it perfect.

Monoproduct Contents

I'd like to offer for your attention a number of criteria which define a 'monoproduct' restaurant:

- A monoproduct restaurant is focused on one dish; other dishes (side dishes or desserts) are only a necessary distraction
- The quality of preparation of this dish is as close to ideal as possible
- The process of preparation of this dish and other technologies are brought to perfection
- The atmosphere (interior design, waiters) focuses the consumer on enjoying the food
- The financial model is extremely stable: energy consumption and staff costs are reduced and the division of labour allows for the raising of productivity.

CONTINUED ...

Monoproduct Goals:

- To offer the customer a dish second to none, a one-off
- To offer the customer a new algorithm: the customer knows which dish he or she wants to taste today and accordingly chooses the restaurant where it is best prepared, and not vice versa
- To make a restaurant famous and popular by providing supreme quality of food preparation
- To create competition with multiproduct restaurants
- To create competition among monoproduct restaurants and contribute to the development of this format.

THREE KEY 'BIG IDEA' FRANCHISOR QUESTIONS

1. Does your brand have an 'elevator-pitch' business model?!
2. Does the financial model provide a high level of *incentive* for prospective franchisees?
3. Is the brand sufficiently *differentiated* to achieve long-term sustainability?

CORNERSTONES

During the process of refining the 'big idea' for the franchised concept, in addition to honing the product and service delivery system, the franchisor will simultaneously develop the key props/foundations of the proposition, namely: the Franchise Agreement and Operations Manual. This activity (often assisted by external professional advice or hired experts) is critical to the whole enterprise because these cornerstone documents will either enhance or degrade the product in the eyes of the 'buyer'. Whilst it is important that the franchisor tightly specifies obligations and the 'rules of the game', a heavy handed and totally one-sided approach will serve as a major detractor to potential franchisees that have plenty of opportunity to look elsewhere for franchising options. In unregulated markets like the UK where voluntary 'codes of conduct' are supposed to act as a break upon unreasonable contracts and behaviour, abuses (in the form of onerous clauses and aggressive application of sanctions) can and do occur. Unsurprisingly, franchises that are set up and operated in such a manner rarely survive due to poor levels of retention and advocacy. But what are the main *qualifiers* for effective Franchise Agreements and Operating Manuals?

- **Franchise Agreement** – the Franchise Agreement is a legally enforceable document between the two parties which specifies duties, rights and obligations within the commercial relationship. Many agreements are fairly 'boilerplate', containing similar clauses – although most are nuanced according to the business model and/or culture of the owner. Successful Franchise Agreements would seem to have a high level of *transparency*, *fairness* and *reasonableness* – particularly with regard to *fees* and important *clauses*:

  - ***Transparent fees –*** although fee structures will evolve over time as the network is developed (particularly with regard to single-multiple transitions) one rule that holds true whatever the context is that effective fee systems are *open* and *transparent*. That is to say, the franchisee has a clear idea of what (s)he is paying for! Generally, four main fees are specified by the Agreement (although different combinations will be contingent on the concept and its business model):

    - *Franchise fee* – this charge should be clearly broken down to demonstrate how it incorporates 'start-up' costs (store fittings, stock, technology, machinery, training, uniforms and marketing) and territorial 'permission to trade'. Sometimes it also covers site finding/negotiation costs and local market insight commissioning by the franchisor. Dependant on the concept this fee can typically vary from £25k–£250k.

    - *Royalty/licence fee* – this fee is usually justified as a payment for central and field-based support services. Charged at between 4% and 20% of sales, this fee will often be capped at a certain turnover threshold. Sometimes franchisors will flex the percentage downwards for inducement purposes (to recruit into the network and/or incentivise single-multiple transitions). Sometimes franchisors that charge for 'tied products' will dispense with this fee altogether.

    - *'Tied product sales'* – a common charge in the UK (less so in the US due to regulatory restrictions), this 'fee' relates to the income that franchisors generate from the provision of 'nominated' company products/services. Transparency here lies in the fact that prospective/existing franchisees can make instant Internet price comparisons on 'similar' products that can be purchased elsewhere. Franchisors that 'gorge' on this income stream by consistently applying above-inflation increases or by failing to return the benefits of upstream efficiencies in the supply chain will encounter a high degree of dissatisfaction amongst their franchisees.

- *Marketing* – some chains that have gained national/regional spread will levy a charge (usually as a percentage of sales) for awareness/promotional marketing (through traditional and digital channels). Often franchisors ameliorate franchisee perception that this fee is just another 'profit stream' for the owner by having its threshold regulated and spend overseen by a joint party Marketing Committee.

- **'Fair' clauses** – as stated, Franchise Agreements have a number of 'boilerplate' clauses which are engineered to protect owners from vicarious liability (not least a duty to observe and enforce the obligations outlined in the Operations Manual – see below). Also, in the UK the franchisor must ensure that these clauses are *enforceable* within contract law but (as importantly) that they are deemed fair by prospective/existing franchisees. Often franchisees will delegate the understanding of the legal minutiae to their lawyers; it is only when they wish to challenge the franchisor or fall into difficulty that they really begin to understand what they have actually signed themselves up to! Franchisors therefore have a duty not to impose agreements that they 'can get away with' but ones that pass the reasonableness test further on down the line. Clauses that usually cause friction between the two parties can be framed sensitively if franchisors ask themselves the following questions:
  - *Territorial rights* – are the anti-encroachment clauses which contain minimum turnover targets (which allow the franchisor to 'carve' up the territory in the event of a breach) fair and reasonable? What level of compensation is given (if any)?
  - *Targets* – are the financial (sales and 'tied product' purchases), operational (minimum standards) and

customer targets (satisfaction and recruitment) imposed from the start in some Agreements or subsidiary documents achievable?

- *Power of audit* – how frequently is the owner allowed to (directly/indirectly and formally/informally) audit the business? What are the sanctions for non-conformance? How powerful are these rights – to what extent can they be abused (such as regaining control of highly profitable businesses)?

- *Renewal/termination* – are automatic rights of renewal or 'first refusal' granted? What are the levels of compensation or payment for asset transfer? In the case of termination for 'final breach' – what are the appeal mechanisms?

- **Operating Manual –** the Franchise Agreement will state that the franchisee is obliged to adhere to the Operating Manual; its blueprint for the way the business should operate. Franchisees will receive training on the content of the Operating Manual during induction and will be offered refresher courses as the content is modified over time (as systems and processes are changed). But what does a good manual look like?

  - ***Clear*** **–** operators are notoriously 'bad readers' so the content of a standard Operating Manual should be easy to understand and use. Typically, it has a number of sections including: *Introduction* (history, purpose/mission, values and contacts), *Market* (concept and typical customers), *Territory Specification*, *Policies and Procedures* (BOH/FOH standards and systems adherence), *Reporting/Administration* (records and accounting), *Statutory Obligations* (health and safety), *Approved Suppliers* ('tied goods' and a selection of nominated suppliers) and *Marketing/Identity* (marketing channels, logos and brochure/promotional 'house styles').

  - ***Interactive/Accessible*** **–** because franchisees (particularly in multiple situations) need to educate other members of staff on their manual's content, the best manuals are also supported by e-learning suites which seek to embed technical knowledge in interesting interactive ways.

  - ***Updateable*** **–** the Operating Manual should be written in such a way that certain sections can be replaced and updated with ease. Rather than being a static document which 'gathers dust' over time, it should be a 'living' embodiment of 'how we do things around here today'!

But if these are the qualifiers for success in constructing the foundations of the franchise, what are the real *differentiators* in securing some form of competitive advantage? These can be summarised as being:

- **Equilibrium** – rather than over-indexing on any one source of fee income it is advisable that franchisors '*spread the load*' for *quality* product, goods and services across three or four streams. This dilutes the chances of being accused of excessive charging for any *single* fee structure.

- **Equity** – essentially, the Franchise Agreement and Operations Manual form the bedrock for an (ideally) long-term, trusting relationship with highly satisfied, motivated franchisees. To some degree, the franchisor can argue that its cornerstone documents serve as protection against extremes and excesses and that 'we rarely enforce x, y or z!' However, if these legally enforceable documents are too draconian (having been constructed purely by lawyers rather than common-sense professionals!) then there will be problems further on down the chain. The documents should stress mutuality and the franchisor's intention to act in 'good faith at all times', *honestly* and openly. Legislate for the worst managerial excesses alongside those of the 'bad' franchisee!

- **Autonomy** – good Franchise Agreements and Operating Manuals not only tell franchisees what they can't do – they also prescribe areas of delegated authority which serve as a licence for autonomous behaviours. Franchisees (especially aspirational/ self-starters) have to feel that there is some 'flexibility with a frame' to express themselves at a local market level.

Case Study 3 – Essential Franchise Cornerstones

John Pratt is co-founder of Hamilton Pratt, a legal firm that specialises in franchising law. John is one of the UK's leading franchise lawyers. During a long and distinguished career he has provided franchise advice to many of the world's most recognised retail brands.

There are usually six documents that underpin the franchise arrangement: two core documents, supported by four subsidiary ones... The two absolutely core documents are the *Franchise Agreement* (FA) and *Operations Manual* (OM)... The FA is written in stone and cannot be altered during the term without the agreement of the franchisee and franchisor; to this extent it can be viewed as a fairly inflexible document which lasts for a long length of time – so getting it right is important! ... The OM is a document that can – and most certainly should – be updated... a major problem (that occurs all too frequently) is that some franchisors 'abandon' the manual, failing to 'bring it up to date' – something that is bad for relationships and the ongoing positioning of the brand...

The four other important 'subsidiary' documents generally include: a *confidentiality agreement* (limiting disclosure of proprietorial information), an *'intent to proceed agreement'* (where the franchisee's agreement to proceed is contingent on sites becoming vacant in a certain area), a *lease agreement* (in cases where the franchisor holds the head lease and sub-lets to the franchisee for a certain period of time; more commonly a 'deed of option' these days) and – increasingly common in North American food brands – an *'area development agreement'*... [H]ere a franchisee is granted rights and obligations to multiple sites in a territory... the reasons behind its increasing usage being the need to recruit franchisees with sufficient 'firepower' who can extend the network quickly, a reduction in franchisor recruitment costs and the financial benefits accruing from one point of contact (simplifies relationships and reduces 'monitoring' costs)...

Getting back to the two cornerstone 'core' documents – what does 'good' look like? With regard to Franchise Agreements, problems

CONTINUED ...

are often caused by well-meaning but overzealous lawyers... in a bid to protect their clients and protect *themselves* from negligence claims further on down the line, some lawyers 'overload' agreements with onerous restrictions and obligations... This not only run contrary to what typical franchise sales documentation talks about ('a partnership', 'mutuality', 'joint interest' etc.), it also is in danger of being struck down on a case-by-case basis by the UK courts... For instance, in February 2013, the High Court ruled in the Yam Seng decision that in relational contracts such as Franchise Agreements the franchisor had certain obligations of 'good faith'... This emerging view of franchise contracts being 'relational' in nature has important consequences, so I believe that it is both prudent – and indeed 'relational' good practice – if franchisors:

- **Focus on the 'Show Stoppers'**... good franchise agreements don't cover every eventuality in the document (covering everything up to and including the invasion of the Martians!)... they focus on the big issues... and franchisors actually ask themselves (to put it 'unenglishly') 'how unonerous can I be'...

- **Emphasise Working Together**... rather than describing duties, responsibilities and obligations in terms of 'you'... talk in terms of 'we'... for instance, 12-month non-compete clauses can be drafted with the opener 'we agree that' rather than 'you will not'! ...

- **Good Faith Obligations...** developing the previous point, making statements such as 'we shall always endeavour to communicate openly and honestly' will not only reinforce the relational rhetoric in the sales brochures but will also create a more conducive 'going in' mentality...

- **Equitable Fees...** there are generally four fees... the *'initial'/ development fee* (this should not include a profit for the franchisor unless the network is highly profitable; otherwise franchises are only being sold for 'initial' fee profit and will collapse at some point)... the *'continuing'/royalty fee* (this should be used to reimburse franchisor operational costs; the average in the UK is 8% of sales turnover)... the *marketing levy* (which is usually about 2% of turnover and should only be spent on marketing)... and, finally, *mark-ups* on (quality!) products/goods the franchisee is

CONTINUED ...

required to buy (these charges should be reflected transparently in the 'continuing fees' section of the agreement... also specifying the retention of rebates is sensible 'relational' thing to do)...

In terms of the Operating Manual – as I said – it is certainly helpful if the franchisor knows it is part of his job description... and certainly his operations/support teams' role to update it! ... this will only improve relations: franchisees like to know what they've got do and how they can do it more effectively...

So in summary I would say that in the UK – due to legal precedent and good commercial practice – Franchise Agreements that emphasise more of a *relational/mutual* ('good faith') approach to defined rights (franchisee access to quality products and goods) and obligations (franchisee system compliance)... will be more resilient and successful in the long term than those that don't... Indeed, I would argue – contrary to some views – that the UK has a very ethical franchised industry... The fact that other regimes are more highly regulated and prescriptive does not mean that they are more benign for franchisees... For instance, pre-contractual disclosure requirements in some territories might seem more protective until you understand that some franchisors can take the view that, if they have disclosed everything, this gives them a licence to be as 'horrible' as they want! ... Although the UK is more 'service' than 'retail orientated' from a franchised perspective (perhaps due to spatial and rental constraints), people are increasingly taking franchises (because of their relatively low failure rate)... certainly, research from the BFA suggests that customers like franchised businesses – surveys indicating that services from franchised firms are better than non-franchised! ...

THREE KEY FRANCHISOR 'CORNERSTONE' QUESTIONS

1. Does your Franchise Agreement include *inclusive* 'good faith' clauses prefaced by *'we* agree' rather than 'you will'?
2. Is the fee structure 'balanced' and explained *honestly/ transparently*?
3. Is your Operations Manual a *quality* document that explains franchisee obligations *simply* and is regularly *updated*?

NETWORK DEVELOPMENT

During the process of designing/refining the concept, initial trials will give some indication regarding ideal territory sizes and site locations. This will help the franchisor to formulate a strategic/business plan which is under-pinned by estimates regarding network growth over a three-to-five-year period. However, scoping and then populating a network with multiple territories is an extremely challenging process. Which areas should the concept cover in the first instance to achieve spatial pre-emption against any competitive threats? Who is the 'ideal' franchisee, how are they located, 'animated' and signed up? In the past, a number of franchise chains (particularly those that have been imported from the US) have failed to reach coverage and scale, not only because they were insufficiently attuned to the idiosyncrasies of the UK market but because – through a lack of market insight – they were launched in inappropriate territories, in the wrong sites with badly matched partners/franchisees. Other problems have arisen due to over-optimistic/aggressive roll-out of plans in which franchisors have played the numbers game, driving network coverage to hit targets, regardless of locational and partner quality.

Given the fact that many roll-out plans have over-exuberant targets (prin-cipally to impress backers/financiers and 'buyers'), what are the main *qualifiers* for building a robust network? Franchisors blessed with a sense of realism and perspective do two things well: *accurate territorial sub-division* (with prioritised areas) and systems that are built around achieving *high sales/recruitment conversion ratios*.

- **Territorial division** – in business format franchising there are few things more important (aside from getting the concept 'big idea' and cornerstones right) than locking down the right territo-ries with the right sites. A mediocre concept in a prime site might succeed – a great concept in a sub-optimal site will struggle. But how is this achieved?
  - *Accurate mapping/Prioritisation* – following the pilot, the franchisor should have a better idea on optimal area size based on demographic density, customer type and transport networks. Lazy approaches to dividing up territories might include crude post/zip-code area carve-ups. Franchisors that use sophisticated *digital mapping software* (which uses algorithms on optimal locations to pinpoint ideal territories) are likely to be more successful. Those that prioritise/rank the

territories they wish to populate first are more likely achieve *network resilience* faster.

- **'Notspot' avoidance** – within any given territory there will be certain locational 'hotspots'. Many franchisors provide assistance (market insight and lease negotiations) to franchisees in locating/procuring sites that fit their specific template/criteria. Indeed, site sign-off by the franchisor is almost always included in the Franchise Agreement. What such assistance is designed to do is avoid '*notspots*': sub-prime locations with poor levels of visibility and traffic.

- **Encroachment protection** – research has consistently demonstrated that 'same concept' encroachment is far more damaging than competitor encroachment (although differences between franchised versus managed 'cannibalisation' have been noted). Delineating exclusive territories (albeit with sales caveats) is sensible – especially in the initial phases of network development.

- **Conversion ratios** – once the foundations of the franchised concept have been put in place and territories have been earmarked 'for sale', the franchisor needs to recruit a vibrant set of franchisees (single, multiple or master). In the initial stages of development this is an extremely difficult process. The proposition is founded more upon promise than reputation! Research demonstrates that new concepts can expect low enquiry/conversion ratios (up to 250:1). Obviously, franchisors can set targets based on their knowledge of competitor conversion rates; but what means do they deploy to gain momentum? Targeting and signing up franchisees from other concepts is one quick route to market given that these operators have already 'taken the leap' and will have more confidence/competence than franchise 'virgins'. To gain traction, however, franchisors must address the *right recruitment channels* with *professional materials*, have *accurate profiles* of the 'ideal' franchisee to conduct *swift interview processes* for 'warm' prospects and – certainly in the early stages at least – be prepared to offer 'signing-on' *incentives/enticements*:

  - **Channels/Materials** – obviously the franchisor must identify the most likely channels for recruitment (web, exhibitions, trade magazines/associations, targeted mailshots etc.) whilst ensuring that its sales/marketing materials are fit for purpose.

Many franchisors have placed a lot of faith in digital channels over the past fifteen years but they will only achieve success if – in addition to 'hard leads' that request further information – they can capture the names of the 'searchers' and follow up with a dialogue. Ensuring that the web presence of the concept has key search words that grab speculative attention is important – but it is also critical that site visits are treated as enquiries and taken through a structured process. In terms of materials, aside from professional visuals/imagery, franchisors must include key hooks/factoids, including: FAQs (costs, prospective returns and territory allocation), testimonials, positive PR/awards, 'day-in-a-life of' etc.

- *Profiling/Interviews* – in order to get the right type of franchisee on-board it is critical that the franchisor has constructed an 'ideal' profile based on *personality* ('entrepreneur' or 'follower'?), *capability* (sector skills?), *situation* (salaried or self-employed?), *motivation* (lifestyle or aspirational) and *resources* (capitalised or borrowing?). This will enable quick decisions to be made during the initial screening and subsequent interview processes. Where a distinct 'fit' has been identified, the franchisor must move swiftly through every part of the process (applying the right 'touches') to build/sustain interest and commitment. This is particularly important in business format franchising given the length of time it can take to finalise lease negotiations on premises.

- *Enticements* – in order to get the prospective franchisee with the correct match on-board (either to pay a deposit or sign a full agreement), franchisors will often 'animate' positive behaviours through offering enticement incentives. In terms of network building, this can be applied to 'converting prospectives' or incentivising existing ones who will aggressively grow the brand – as the excerpt below demonstrates.

  ... Papa John's franchisee plans five sites thanks to incentives: Papa John's franchisee Steve Mullarkey, who recently opened a Warrington store, has signed up to open five more outlets using the support of the company's 2014 franchise incentive scheme. Mullarkey, who has a background in catering, will be opening the new outlets across the North West with a store in St Helens planned for launch in the coming months. The chain's latest franchisee incentive deal, announced last month as its 'biggest and best' franchise incentive scheme, applies to new stores in Wales, the Midlands, the North East, the North West and Scotland with 12-month royalty breaks available to those that open stores before July 2014, and a nine-month royalty break for stores opened before the end of 2014. As part of the scheme, new franchisees will also have access to free oven and refrigerator equipment, royalty holiday and £10,000 worth of marketing spend. Mullarkey said: 'My research showed that Papa John's was very simply better than the competition. Papa John's is an exciting company and committed to growth. The head-office staff's enthusiasm for the future is impressive, they really believe this company is going places and I have to agree. I aim to open between ten to 15 Papa John's over the next five years.' (Charity, 2014a)

In spite of the extract above – which seems to advocate extending a network through high levels of incentivisation in a blaze of publicity – it is not advisable to 'force' system growth at any cost. Blatant 'giveaways' might betray the weakness of the proposition and are apt to demotivate existing partners who joined on less-favourable terms. The *differentiators* for network development suggest a more cautious approach yields better returns through *optimising rather than maximising*, *judicious clawbacks* and *patient churn*.

- **Optimisation NOT maximisation** – in order to 'fill spaces' on the map, seek rapid national/regional coverage and attract 'excited' partners, it is tempting for franchisors to 'sell' large territories. Franchisors – with high levels of estate development *expertise* – are more likely to grant smaller areas (in order of attractiveness) that have been scientifically scoped/researched for the prospects for success (see case study below).

- **Judicious enticements** – granting 'special deals' to prospective/existing (multiple) franchisees is a useful way of rapidly extending the network. After all, franchisees are businessmen who like to feel that they have negotiated some 'material advantage' or 'inside edge'. But as stated above, franchisors who apply a scatter-gun approach to incentivisation (different levels of incentives for different partners) will most likely build resentment amongst their existing franchised community. Taking exclusive, rather than *inclusive* approaches will invariably misfire in the end.

- **Reasonable clawbacks** – once recruited/installed, where franchisees have failed to meet their territory targets, franchisors are entitled (in most circumstances) to clawback parts of the territory to 'sell on'. This is a useful method of building the network (especially when it approaches maturity) but franchisors must be careful not to undermine trust in the wider network by instituting wholesale 'landgrabs'.

Case Study 4 – Mid-Scale Network Development at Domino's Pizza Group (DPG)

Maurice Abboudi is a serial casual dining entrepreneur (Famous Moe's Pizza, Pizza Lupa and K10 Restaurants) who was Head of Business Development (responsible for property and franchising) for DPG UK during a critical phase of its network growth from approximately 200 to 330 stores.

Having sold my first business, Famous Moe's Pizza (12 Units), I was approached by Domino's to become Head of Business Development at a very interesting stage of their development. At the time, the master franchise for the company in the UK – which had experienced significant ups and downs during the '80s and '90s – had been bought by the Halpern brothers. They had built strong foundations and then hired Stephen Helmsley (a visionary, energetic and very focused corporate leader) to turn it around (constructing a better supply chain, building a commissary, developing operations and setting minimum OER standards). Part of this revival process involved more professional and scientific network development... previously, under the old system, territories had been divided up into around 50,000 households and 15-minute drive times... or circles had been drawn around towns in a fairly unsophisticated way... indeed, it was rumoured that in the early days of the franchise the first denominated territories were shaped around the names of towns that had football teams! ... Of course, in those days organisations had no GPS or computer systems and so crude 'hand-processed' methods were used to subdivide territories! When I joined DPG we had about 200 stores – usually the tipping point

CONTINUED ...

for brand scale in the UK. The challenge was to manage profitable network growth not only by identifying new territories but optimising the territories that were already assigned – some were too large and 'under leveraged', offering far greater potential… So how did we go about doing this?

What became quite clear to us in Business Development was that the 'territorial integrity' of the company was (for historic reasons) unbalanced… We had a strong hypothesis that certain territories could take more sites with tighter demographics/drive times (say 15–25,000 people and 8-minute drive times) and that reducing territory sizes would actually increase sales rather than dilute them! … But first we needed to prove it and then we needed to go about systematically reconfiguring the estate… *In terms of proof, we included a couple of franchisees in the trial process*… [and] scientifically evaluated their territories… Through '*heat mapping*' we located where their existing customers were located and identified the '*golden mile*' around their stores… then using this data together with demographic analysis, housing density/ownership (existing/proposed) and road access we identified other unexploited 'golden miles' in their territories that could take a store… As we split the territories, we found that stores achieved better productivity and delivery speeds, leading to vastly improved repeat business, with local awareness of the brand being significantly enhanced… Having proved it could work, we then turned our attention to the wider estate… which 10-year agreements were coming up for renewal? … could these territories be sub-divided into more effective clusters? … As renewal dates approached, although we gave most of the existing franchisees the first 'right of refusal' (if they had achieved a minimum 3* OER ratings – since increased to 4*)… the new agreements had 'rights to expansion' clauses defining specific territorial rights/obligations (such as mandatory store targets)… Because we had proven that 'smaller was better', many franchisees took the 'leap of faith'… *through the provision of exceptional data, expertise and back up*… and renewed on different terms…

One of the reasons why our stores were able to service smaller areas more effectively at this time was due to the huge advances

CONTINUED …

in operational efficiency... the organisation improved its approach to *volume and capacity management*... driving throughputs by improvements in taking orders, on-site production processes and delivery... For instance, Islington was a problem territory taking £3k p.w. ... the company lent an Assistant Manager the money to buy the franchise... he put in about twelve phone lines, an extra deck in the oven, employed an additional 12–15 drivers and leafleted 10,000 households per week... the result? ... capacity constraints had been removed and the store became one of the most successful in the system! ... Today stores generate 70% of their orders digitally (saving on labour), have three oven decks and anything between 20–30 drivers! ... The estate has been dramatically reconfigured with fewer franchisees running more stores (180:300 ratio in the noughties – 110:800 today) ... This has increased the *symbiotic and interdependent relationship* between DPG and its franchisees (two of which have over 100 stores)... it has meant that DPG is able to concentrate on product quality and digital innovation whilst its franchisees concentrate on operational execution! ... Today, it can be said – *DPG does not sell franchises, it awards them!* ...

THREE KEY 'NETWORK DEVELOPMENT' FRANCHISOR QUESTIONS

1. Do you have sufficient *expertise* in your 'Network Development' team to subdivide areas/territories, locate hotspots ('golden miles') and churn the estate?

2. Does 'brand attractiveness' or generous incentivisation drive franchise sales? (The former is more viable than the latter!)

3. Are you decreasing the cost of operations and (simultaneously) increasing the quality of your estate by getting the 'best' franchisees to take on more stores?

CHAPTER SUMMARY

This chapter has summarised how franchisors can win through *designing* their product and rolling it out on a considered, systematic basis. But what are the key underlying determinants of success? In essence, franchisors will win if they achieve a blend of **transactional** and **relational** elements of their exchange with franchisees. To this extent, the **three major case study** narratives presented above validate the **dominant archetypes of exchange** between business partners – money, product/goods, services, love, information and status (Foa and Foa 1974, 1980) – as being particularly significant in ensuring mutual success. **Transactional exchange** is satisfied by the 'big idea' (Burger & Lobster) *incentivising* franchisees through a 'simple… extremely stable business model' (monetary exchange), 'cornerstone' documents of the franchise (Hamilton Pratt) undertaking to provide '*quality* product/goods' in 'good faith' (product and goods exchange) and the 'network development' (Domino's) process providing franchisees with 'exceptional data, *expertise* and back-up' to extend their portfolios (services exchange). **Relational exchange** is aided through the 'big idea' (Burger & Lobster) gaining wide stakeholder *recognition* through 'fame and popularity' (love exchange), the 'cornerstone documents' (John Pratt) being 'open and *honest*' (information exchange) and 'network development' (Domino's) '*including* franchisees' in trials and 'awarding' successful operators with more units/territories (status exchange). But how do franchisors execute their 'product promise' on a day-to-day basis? This is addressed by the next chapter, which deals with delivery.

DELIVERY

The previous chapter addressed the principles of franchised business format *design*, outlining how 'winning' franchisors conceived/tested their formatted concept, refined the fundamental props that underpinned their enterprise and went about building a robust network. But how do they go about *delivering* and maintaining industrial standardisation within their business – maintaining high levels of quality and consistency that benefit all stakeholders? This chapter will examine how they engage successfully in this pursuit by discussing *qualifiers* and *differentiators* which relate to *support and service* infrastructure/activity, 'hard' formal control mechanisms (*franchisor control systems* – FCS) and 'soft' ideological control methods (*binding values*).

SUPPORT STRUCTURE AND SERVICES

One of the key selling points made by most franchisors in their sales brochures/literature is the level of support infrastructure that lies behind their franchised proposition. By highlighting this as a key feature, they are signalling to prospective franchisees that they have the *expert resources* in place to facilitate joint business success and an excellent working *relationship*! The problem for new franchisors, however, is judging at what pace they put in place costly head office and field-based staff. Often the promises they make relating to comprehensive support services bear no resemblance to reality. By contrast, organisations that are developing a franchised product out of a managed concept are, on the face of it, in a more advantageous position because they already have a central infrastructure in place. However, although existing staff will be fully conversant with operating the brand in a managed context, they are likely to lack tacit knowledge relating to how they should support it as a franchised product. Given the fact that (as stated in 'Cornerstones' in the previous chapter) franchisors often justify licence fees as being payments for support and services, what are the main *qualifiers* and *differentiators* with regards to this area? With regard to the former, three overarching principles will govern effectiveness: *integration, added value* and *communication.*

- **Integrated support infrastructure** – franchises evolving from a single business face a number of questions: how should they design their support architecture, in what order of priority do they build in personnel and what type of staff are likely to provide value added?

  - *Coherence* – the architecture of the support structure must be aligned with the concept and its blueprint. For instance, business formats that rely heavily on generating revenue through 'tied products' must have an appropriate sourcing and supply chain arm.

  - *Sequencing* – in the early days of building the franchised product, franchisors will limit their fixed overhead through using consultants for specialist services (finance, property, legal, marketing and sales/enquiry handling) and (where possible) existing staff in owned stores for operational functions (training, auditing and business advice). As the franchised brand gains momentum, full-time staff are co-opted in different orders of priority according to the 'gravity' of the brand. A common mistake made by franchisors – through an obsession with the product itself – is inattention to installing effective financial capability that generates essential management information; particularly in the early days when (typically) capital is scarce and cash flows are tight.

  - *Capability* – whether recruiting consultants, interims, temporary or full-time staff the franchisor, would be wise to select as many 'franchised veterans' as possible. One way of gaining access to good people can be achieved through appointing non-executives with extensive franchised-industry experience. In most instances it is impossible to 'load up' at all levels with support staff with previous franchised experience so what generic qualities (aside from specific professional skills) are needed by support functionaries? Attributes that are useful within this environment include a positive attitude, high levels of emotional intelligence (self-knowledge, resilience and empathy), good communication skills and what might be termed 'mature worldliness' (nous and guile).

- **Added-value services** – the extent to which central/field-based services add value to their businesses is likely to have a strong effect upon franchisee *satisfaction*. Indeed, those that have transitioned through the lifecycle from being 'compliant' (new starter), 'committed' (business builder) to 'challenger' (mature operator) are less likely to be 'difficult' in the latter phase of the cycle if they feel that the services they are being offered continue to drive sources of added value. But what are the principal services offered by business format franchises?

  - *Financial* – such as start-up and ongoing financial reports/information. Offering 'basic' small-business advice (funding, registering etc.) in the early days is highly valuable to new entrants with no prior independent business experience.

  - *Property/IT* – usually includes site finding, fit-out (machines, BOH/FOH systems etc.) and maintenance assistance/advice. Effective IT support, lying behind robust/integrated systems, will be highly valued by franchisees.

  - *Operational execution* – incorporating field-based advice, training and monitoring from Franchised Support Managers (FSMs) and field trainers, auditors etc. This is likely to be intensive in the franchisee's early days (following their induction/immersion), tailing off into a standardised routine of meetings, audits and training refreshers/updates. Operational support that drives operational efficiency relentlessly (skills, deployment, productivity, service etc.) will be received well by franchisees.

  - *Supply chain* – purchasing processes that seek to limit both 'tied' and approved product inflation and/or source cheaper products that can be sold at a higher margin are vital for sustained good relations.

  - *Marketing/promotions* – 'glocal' marketing/promotions mechanisms that drive added-value awareness and traffic (during specific seasons, key dates and 'slack' timeslots) are critically important services (particularly when it constitutes a specific fee). Ensuring that franchisees do not get trapped in 'time-bomb' promotional mechanics that grow sales for the franchisor but dilute franchisee margin is vital for long-term network harmony.

  - *Help desk/administration* – the provision of help-desk services and an effective administrative structure that enable franchisees to resolve issues on maintenance, systems, supply chain, administrative/financial queries and so forth will greatly aid relations between both parties. Such services will free up capacity for field-based personnel such as FSMs to concentrate upon providing added value on the front line.

- **Communications** – alongside the provision of tangible support and services that provide the franchisee with the wherewithal to get the job done 'with no excuses' – as one respondent during the course of this research stated – the provision/maintenance of excellent communication *processes* and *content* is an essential service ingredient, as the excerpt below illustrates:

> **Marston's boosts online communication for franchisees:**
> Marston's has developed its online communications tools to offer greater support to its franchisees. This month sees the launch of a quarterly video news update service and also an online forum for Marston's franchise members, both housed on Marston's central communications system. Celene Normoyle, franchise development manager for Marston's, said: 'Our video news programmes provide a round-up of the key news and developments from within the franchise estate and wider business. Internal communication has a fundamental role to play in strengthening our franchise relationships and we wanted to do this in a fun and engaging way. Of course, this doesn't take away from our daily communications with franchisees, but we were keen to be creative and move away from more traditional channels such as newsletters and emails. Going forward the video news programmes will be released on a quarterly basis and will include such things as key trading results, new franchisees into the network, franchisee achievements and recognition for creative sales activity, as well as updates from a range of support departments including menu development, marketing services and training. The online forum will enable franchisees to communicate more freely with one another, irrespective of location, with a representative for the franchise management team actively participating in discussions and answering questions where required'.
>
> (Charity 2014b)

But what differentiates good franchisor support structures and services? Two main attributes stand out, namely **high levels of co-operation amongst support personnel** and **rapid response services**:

- **Support co-operation** – in order to run a successful network, support functions combine their *expertise* and work together not only to improve their levels of service delivery but also their level of product and franchisee knowledge/insight. To the latter point, given that many support services might 'touch' the franchisee at any given time, it is expeditious for organisations to have a 'universal log' that can be updated by support staff detailing their contact with franchisees. Regular meetings between field and critical support functions are also essential to promote intelligence gathering/dissemination.

- **Service response** – one major detractor in relations – highlighted in numerous franchisee surveys on internal 'service provision' – is a slow response to 'resolve issues' by franchisor personnel. Sometimes franchisees might exhaust the patience of support staff through needy behaviours and 'game play' but this does not excuse universal avoidance behaviours (based on extreme cynicism) at the centre or in the field. It's better to *recognise* franchisee requests – respond and say 'no' if necessary – than not to respond at all.

Case Study 5 – Successful Managed-to-Franchised Model Transition within Budgens

Paul Daynes held executive positions with Musgrave UK (Budgens and Londis) and BP Forecourt Retail. Currently he is Group HR Director for St Gobain Building Distribution UK and Ireland (Jewson, Grahams, Minster, International Timber) the UK's largest builders merchants.

Musgrave were a family-owned, franchised food-retail business which had successfully built supermarket (Supervalu) and convenience (Centra) franchised concepts within its core Irish market. Gaining either of these franchises in Ireland was looked upon as

CONTINUED ...

being highly valuable – Musgrave deployed extremely generous terms... they imposed no caps on how much franchisees could earn – believing that tying franchisees in 'through chains of gold' was mutually beneficial to both parties – although they deliberately restricted the number of stores that franchisees could own to about three proximal sites... Looking to expand out of Ireland, they analysed a number of international opportunities before settling on the UK, where a listed, managed food-retail chain called Budgens, based mainly in the affluent south east, was up for sale... Although Budgens had been trialling some franchised sites, Musgrave – having bought the chain for (what was at the time) a hefty consideration – went about converting *all* the sites to franchised agreements... They were extremely successful in doing so – subsequently purchasing the Londis convenience chain to sit alongside the Budgens supermarkets, mirroring their Irish model... But what was the managed-to-franchised transition *process* at Budgens and why was it so *successful*?

In terms of *process*, what they did was properly to establish proof of concept through piloting/trialling the concept over about 20 sites... refining the concept (concentrating on 'fresh' and 'quality'), understanding how the 'cornerstone' aspects of the deal could work (legals, fees, operating manual etc.) and what support services were required for an efficient operation... With regards to support services, they expertly refined two 'hygiene' aspects of the operation: *robust IT platforms* (for BOH ordering/replenishment and FOH sales reporting) and *'top draw' logistics systems* (that focused upon delivering 'right product, right quality, right time')... They also provided excellent local marketing and training support packages, professional field-based support and a list of recommended suppliers that could provide maintenance, refurbishment, payroll and legal support etc. ... In terms of recruitment, many of the first franchisees were actually Budgens employees (either GMs, field or centrally based staff) who were steeped in the differentiated 'fresh'-based ethos of the brand...

Why was the transition a *success*? ... First, because it was a well-planned/executed project that focused upon creating a differentiated

CONTINUED ...

'quality food retail' franchise (with a focus upon quality fresh, chilled and ambient)... Second, because of Musgrave's experience and heritage, they were able to *transition people from a managed to a franchised mindset*. Central staff had to accept that, due to the new business model (with a slimmer P&L and clients paying for services), fewer people had to operate more quickly/efficiently and the Budgens personnel who took the franchises had to realise that they had to do a lot more independently and/or pay for certain services! ... Third, they encouraged all stakeholders (franchisees, customers and suppliers) to attach and engage with the brand by having a *'local' focus*; insisting that franchisees placed their name on the brand fascias (e.g. Warners's Budgens) in recognition of the key role of the owner/proprietor, encouraging community activity and (some) local quality-product sourcing backed up by slick marketing/sourcing mechanics... Fourth – and most importantly perhaps – they concentrated on *creating great relationships* with their franchisees... the starting point being that Musgrave allowed franchisees to buy the original managed properties on generous terms; meaning that if the agreement lapsed after the 10-year term, franchisees had a valuable asset that they could sell or convert into another concept... Also, Musgrave had a an astonishingly frank and benevolent *core value of 'don't be greedy'*... as a family-run business they believed in long-term sustainable relationships with their franchisees based on mutual respect founded upon a fair 'division of the spoils'... as I said, Musgrave were quite keen to lock their franchisees in with 'chains of gold' so that they didn't move to other symbol franchised groups and – because of the high value of the franchise – operated the franchise to unbelievably high standards (a must, given the 'fresh quality' ethos of the brand)... I still know several of the original 'corporate franchisees' today who are still there, have done extremely well out of the arrangement and are (still) unbelievably committed to the franchisor and the brand! ...

THREE KEY 'SUPPORT STRUCTURE AND SERVICES' FRANCHISOR QUESTIONS

1. Does your support team have sufficient *expertise*/capability to provide a quality service (speed/value-added) to franchisees?

2. Do your support services co-operate amongst one another to provide a *quality* 'joined-up' approach?

3. Is your support team cognisant of both the national and *local* demands of the brand/operators?

FRANCHISOR CONTROL SYSTEMS (FCS)

Franchisor control systems (measures, KPIs, reporting and audits) are a vitally important means for the franchisor to *monitor* adherence to the blueprint and drive operational excellence. The principal objective of business format franchising is to establish a network of stores which attract both local and mobile customers who value their consistency and reliability. Any deviation from standards in the form of 'shirking' or 'free-riding' behaviour by franchisees (or their managers in multiple operations) can seriously compromise the reputation of the concept. Obviously, the Operations Manual serves as the template which, theoretically, franchisees are legally obligated to execute, through signing the Franchise Agreement; failure to do so resulting in detrimental consequences. Contained within the Operations Manual are a number of targets and specifications-based 'monitoring' brand standards which – if the franchisee achieves them seamlessly – will lead to certainty of positive outcomes (quality, safety, service, sales etc.) for the franchisor. However, driving compliance and conformance 'at a distance' is problematic for the franchisor. 'Opportunistic' franchisees seeking to maximise profits can 'cut corners' whilst benefiting from the efforts of others in the wider network. Their geographical detachment from the centre and lack of daily direct supervision affords them protection from scrutiny. So what do good FCSs look like? What are the main *qualifiers* for success and what are the ultimate *differentiators*?

The main qualifiers for effective FCSs include relevance, accuracy, timeliness, communication/understanding and robust monitoring/correction:

- **Relevant measures** – the starting point for successful FCSs is the construction of a set of measures that drive behaviours that achieve positive outcomes for the concept. Common errors include obsessing with outputs to the exclusion of important 'input drivers' and failing to put the customer at the heart of measurement systems. How is this rectified?
  - *Customer first* – understanding what the customer values/ expects from the concept is vitally important in designing

appropriate FCSs. If the customer values quality, speed and affordability then franchisors must isolate these variables and relentlessly focus upon increasing perception/satisfaction in these areas (through user/lapsed/non-user tracking, third-party mystery customer visits, on-line surveys/feedback, complaint analysis etc.).

- *Input/output linkages* – obviously the franchisor will set measures for *financial* outputs (sales and transactions) but it is the degree to which (s)he also has a suite of input measures that are empirically linked to driving these outputs which is of greatest importance. Hence, *customer* measurement (as stated above) along with 'linked' *operational* factors (BOH/FOH standards/systems compliance) are vital components of successful FCSs. Several franchised concepts also insist (in spite of not directly employing franchise store personnel directly) on having access to store-level *people* data (skills, stability, turnover, satisfaction, absence, disciplinaries etc.) which assists a 'balanced' view of performance outcomes.

- **Sensible targets** – whilst some targets are immutable (driven by legislation and legal requirements), others relating to financial, customer, operational and people performance are guided by the discretion of the franchisor. These targets should be stretching, aspirational and (ultimately) achievable rather than impossibly unreachable.

- **Clear/accurate/timely reporting** – providing central and local reporting systems that are *easy to use* (not tying up too much administrative time), *understandable* (including pictorial dashboards/graphs as well as figures), *accurate* (uncorrupted by being drawn off multiple 'unconnected' platforms/spreadsheets) and *timely* (by session, day, week, month, quarter etc.) will aid FCS effectiveness.

- **Stringent checking/correction** – in terms of 'following up' and monitoring, field-based personnel such as FSMs will hold regular mandated business performance/planning reviews with franchisees. Operational execution and adherence to the blueprint will be checked regularly through formal (announced) and spontaneous (unannounced) audits conducted by multiple parties (field operatives, central compliance and third parties). Often, inconsistent FCS data will flag up sites that might be compromising the network, with audits being drawn towards miscreants who are 'punished' accordingly (financial penalties, 'warnings' or termination). Franchisors with more nous will have 'early warning systems' that detect those that are heading for major problems and seek to resolve/correct these issues in a professional, supportive and sympathetic manner. Such an approach is more likely to result in fewer contested exits.

- **Regular communications** – another means of shaping behaviour lies in internally publicising comparative performance through regular league tables (focussing upon sales, operational and customer performance) which are disclosed in communications updates (e-newsletters, regional/national meetings and award ceremonies). Franchisees are naturally competitive; being and staying at the top or moving out of the lower quartile is a matter of ego-driven pride!

If these are the base qualifiers for FCS effectiveness, what are the key differentiators that really drive performance? Three areas stand out: the provision not just of data but *actionable insights*, *incentives* that extend beyond definitions of compliance and cool *judgement/common sense* surrounding monitoring and correction.

- **Actionable insights** – the point that is made above about successful FCSs incorporating 'joined-up' inputs and outputs needs extending. It is only through identifying specific linkages/dependencies that *lead to* actionable insights that FCSs prove their worth. For instance, if sales and transactions are down, there could be a multiplicity of reasons; but what are the major dependencies within this franchised concept? If customer service is at fault, which aspect is most important – product quality, speed, politeness and/or knowledge? What are the causes of these defects? Does the store have high levels of turnover which are connected to poor morale, linked to poor leadership (communications, training and development)? If so, what actions need to be taken: leadership coaching and/or 'local' HRM systems? The point here being that, of themselves, FCSs are not solutions; they merely provide the information and insights to apply appropriate remedies.
- **Incentives** – the economic academic literature referred to in the Introduction postulates that mutual incentives in the franchised contract exist for both parties, reduced monitoring costs for the franchisor and conformance-related contract continuity for the

franchisee. However, in normative terms, franchisors also use *incentives* as behavioural drivers; for example, setting licensing-fee caps dependant on reaching sales targets or granting 'off-invoice laddered discounts' for tied-product purchases. Hence aspects of FCSs can be used as 'carrots' as well as 'sticks'.

- **'Circle of compromise'** – at times there will be extremely valid reasons for non-conformance to prescribed measures or targets. With the exception of those which are legally prescribed, the franchisor's field operatives might make *'honest'* exceptions due to extenuating circumstances (such as illness or competitor poaching). Also non-compliance can result from the franchisor's actions, such as: inability to supply, faulty promotions and systems breakdowns. In such circumstances, ignoring minor breaches that fall within the 'circle of compromise' can build reciprocity and indebtedness, strengthening the relationship between the two parties. Indeed, franchisors that *only* apply transactional 'coercive/positional' as opposed to relational 'expert/referent' power are ultimately likely to fail.

Case Study 6 – Franchise Control Systems in Citroen

Bryn Thomas is Finance Director at Citroen UK (14 managed and 187 franchised dealerships) having been previously Franchising Director, Director of Sales Programmes and an area manager (managed and franchised) for Peugeot. In 2013, the Citroen DS3 was awarded best 'super mini' status by the influential JD Power survey.

In Citroen UK, we have honest and accurate real-time 'output' and 'input' data/information systems in place to ensure that the sales and aftersales performance of our franchised network (SUF and MUF) is properly monitored and 'animated'. The start point is agreeing *outputs* with dealerships, namely – agreeing volume sales targets on an annual basis. This is a *consultation* process where our Zone Managers responsible for 8–10 dealerships look

CONTINUED ...

at the previous year's trading, examine the customer profile in the immediate area and examine calendar events in the new financial year (national promotions and new launches), agreeing contractual numbers with the franchisee. Laddered financial incentives are applied for monthly sales (from 80–120+% of target) with 'calendarisation' factors being applied (such as March and September new registration months). However, in my view it is the 'input' systems that drive sales 'outcomes' – customer service index (CSI), staff competency matrices, rolling audits and communications – which are the most vital factor in our FCS…

In Citroen, the CSI is one of the most important behavioural drivers, underpinning our customer service ethos… it looks at two main areas: 'lead management' and 'customer experience at the point of purchase'. In terms of lead management, we measure 'speed of response', requiring a minimum of 85% of all enquiries (through whichever channel) to be addressed within 8 hours. This data is gathered both electronically and though prospect customer 'check backs'/questionnaires. Customer experiences at the point of purchase are measured by post-negotiation/sale questionnaires (how easy was it to park, did the receptionist greet you, were you offered finance or a test drive? etc.). Every six months we analyse the CSI results for each dealership and – if they pass the minimum thresholds – pay out incentives to the best performers (either as a % of sales or £ per car sold). Like the rest of the industry, we are also looking at 'real-time' customer data systems (such as customer feedback sites directly on dealer websites) that will give instant (actionable) feedback…

In addition to the CSI, we also have other 'input' systems that mould desired behaviours such as staff competency measurement, audits and targeted communications. In the case of competencies, we measure the knowledge and skills of all our managed/franchised dealership personnel to assess gaps that require training and development. We also conduct a rolling cycle of formal audits that check that franchisees are at least complying with minimum brand standards (both financial and environmental)… these are conducted by a mixture of external personnel (i.e. financial auditors), head-office

CONTINUED …

staff and field-based managers... The one thing I would say about audits being conducted by field personnel is that they can sometimes be 'commercially conflicted' if the performance of the branch is good but its standards fall below required parameters! ... Finally, we also motivate our franchisees through regular communications – both written and face to face – which have plenty of league tables, highlighting the best (and worst!) performers (drawing on the competitive nature of franchisees)... Our annual 'Citroen Award for Excellence' is in an incredible motivator...

Having done many of the financial, commercial and field-support roles in Peugeot Citroen, I would say that control systems work when they are transparent and fair... We monitor our relationships with our franchisees independently through National Franchise Dealer Association surveys (measuring openness, responsiveness and flexibility) which give a strong indication as to what we are getting right and wrong... informing our approaches and practices going forwards... But I would also add that applying controls is not necessarily the same within SUFs and MUFs – some of our larger MUFs are multi-franchise dealerships where we have more of a 'head office to head office' relationship where they have their own 'duplicated' structures, systems and processes in place... The best franchisees also make sure that incentives that we put in place 'flow down' to their key personnel (certainly on new sales and CSI scores)... and the best field-based managers do apply controls and incentives without favouritism, having the judgement and wisdom to make the right calls if things are being done incorrectly (such as poor local marketing execution)... After all, this is a relationship between two parties where if *'you do a, b, c – I'll do x, y, z!'* does operate (i.e. delivering more car registrations at a certain time will result in enhanced incentives/support)...

THREE KEY 'FRANCHISE CONTROL SYSTEMS' FRANCHISOR QUESTIONS

1. Do your measurement/monitoring systems start with the customer? (That is to say, are they measuring the things of greatest importance to your end users?)

2. Do you have simple, accurate and insightful data that is conveyed to franchisees in real time?

3. Are your business KPIs backed up by 'animating' *incentives* that shape/drive the right behaviours?

BINDING VALUES

Alongside Franchise Control Systems (FCS) – measurement/monitoring practices which might be termed as hard *bureaucratic controls* – successful franchisors develop a soft *socio-ideological* approach exemplified through a 'values system' which mandates a set of required behaviours that are the basis for practical/ethical action. These are intended to shape attitudes and guide practices that provide the moral standards for 'permissible' conduct within the network. In some instances – most pertinently within international contexts – these serve as a corrective against ingrained personal or cultural values which might subvert (contrary to franchisor wishes) how people are treated and/or day-to-day business is transacted. To this extent, organisational values require *bounded* statements of 'the way we do things around here' in order to ensure that, in the absence of explicit instructions, franchisees and their staff are *programmed* 'to do the right thing' in most circumstances, rather than falling back on pre-learnt defective behaviours.

The attraction of binding values systems is that they are a cheaper form of control mechanism than bureaucratic FCSs. Also, given the fact that, as one respondent said, 'you can't take the Operations Manual onto the trading floor', they provide the franchisor with some comfort that franchisees act properly in most circumstances – thereby protecting the integrity/reputation of the brand. But what are the main qualifiers and differentiators of binding values systems? On the whole, the basic features of successful binding values include:

- **Coherent logic** – the starting point for successful values systems (the 'how') is resonance with 'what' the brand stands for and 'why' it exists (see the 'Big Idea' section of Chapter 2). They are also memorable and connected with founder purpose and values:
  - *Simplicity* – memorability stems from simplicity! For instance, Burberry's values of 'protect, inspire, explore' implicitly exhort all members of the network (both managed and licensed) to

protect the brand's reputation in everything they do, *inspire* one another to greater heights of achievement and *explore* ways of developing and extending the brand.

- '*Brand archaeology*' – values derived from the founder, bolstered by stories/legends relating to 'the way we act around here', are a form of 'brand archaeology' that will resonate strongly at all levels. For instance, Ray Kroc's 'quality, value, service and cleanliness' devised over fifty years ago still guide behaviours within McDonald's today.

- **Intrinsic alignment** – in order to ensure that values are maintained/sustained throughout the network, successful franchisors seek intrinsic alignment between stakeholders through:

  - *Recruitment/immersion* – franchisors actively test the 'value set' of recruits (centre, field and network) to establish 'fit'. Intensive induction training is designed to 'socialise' and immerse new members in the values of the organisation.

  - *Communication* – all internal/external communications is crafted around values for resonance. In particular, it is important that the values of the franchised organisation extend beyond internal boundaries to connect with external stakeholders not only to strengthen the identity of the brand but reinforce their importance to corporate staff and the network.

  - *Modelling* – values are modelled in both 'word and deed' by leaders within the franchised brand. They make a conscious effort to act as standard bearers and exemplars for their franchise's values even when (in an international context perhaps) they run counter to extant local cultural norms: for instance, basing network appointments on capability rather than relationships in high-context societies.

- **Intentional/purposeful behaviours** – major consequences of coherent value sets with a high degree of intrinsic alignment are intentional/purposeful behaviours. That is to say, franchisors can guarantee that members of the network will act in 'values-led synchronicity' due to 'cultural binds'. In international contexts, ensuring that corporate values (such as openness and meritocracy) transcend debilitating societal norms (such as self-protective leadership and nepotism) can deliver competitive advantage for the franchisor.

But what are the real differentiators for successful values systems within franchised propositions? Two elements stand out: *stewardship* of 'binding values' not only by franchisors but franchisees themselves and, connected to this, *self-regulating* behaviours that resolve any systemic breaches within the network.

- **Stewardship** – whilst it is taken as read that the franchisor's 'corporate staff' should be the standard bearers for the concept's *all-inclusive* values, academics have noted that this is not always the case:

    a recurring franchisee narrative views the franchisor as a perpetu- ally unstable and unpredictable exchange partner while long-time franchisees and the associations they constitute view themselves as legitimate stewards of the brand...

    (Lawrence and Kaufmann 2011: 286)

Whilst the franchisor's managers might change frequently over time – prompting alterations in strategic direction – the permanence of 'early adopter' franchisees throws up an interesting conundrum. Who are the real guardians of the brand and its values? In strong franchises, the stewardship of the brand's values – a tacit understanding of its 'real DNA' – reaches beyond management. Hence, long-serving franchisees often regard themselves as 'moral guardians' juxtaposed against short-term managerialism: a tension that can result in positive outcomes for the brand over time.

- **Self-regulation** – in addition, 'values buy-in' by successful franchisees can result in self-regulating behaviours where Franchisee Associations and special committees support vigorous management action against rogue members of the network. Instances of 'good' franchisees whistleblowing destructive behaviour by other members, which threatens the integrity/*quality* of the brand, is another positive outcome of extremely successful 'binding values' systems.

Case Study 7 – Binding Values at the YHA

Jerry Robinson is National Operations Director at the Youth Hostel Association, a charitable organisation that provides affordable urban and rural accommodation for young people (individuals, groups and families) through a network of 130 managed and 50 enterprise (franchised) units. Jerry formerly held senior executive positions with a number of large hospitality organisations and graduated with an MSc (with distinction) in Multi-Unit Leadership and Strategy from BCU in 2013.

I have just completed an intensive tour of the YHA estate, immersing myself in its culture and acquainting myself with its operations and people... They say that first impressions are lasting ones and one of the main things that has struck me – particularly given my previous commercial background – is the way that (unlike some corporates) the values that underpin the organisation and bind it together are not rhetoric: they are sincerely held by all members of the organisation at all levels in both managed and franchised contexts... *What* are these values, *how* are they brought alive and perpetuated and *what* are their outcomes? ...

- **YHA Values** – the YHA's mission is to *'inspire'* young people... this is backed up by four strategic goals (clustered around people & teams, customers & service, development & partnerships and financial sustainability & growth) which are underpinned by six core values: sustainability, passion, innovation, responsibility, inclusivity and trust... Through close observation there are three that strike me as being particularly resonant throughout the organisation... *sustainability*: achieving environmental longevity *and* network resilience... *inclusivity*: valuing diversity (class, race, nationality and ability) *and* contributing to societal cohesion... *trust*: maintaining a reputation for securing the safety *and* well-being of young people when they are entrusted to us...

- **Perpetuation/Reinforcement** – in my view, the way in which the values are embedded and perpetuated over both the managed and franchised estate is derived from three sources... First, the CEO and her senior leadership team are extremely

CONTINUED ...

'non-hierarchical' and visible within the business, regularly visiting hostels and communicating directly with managers/franchisees (business briefings, award ceremonies, family events etc.)... Also (and crucially in my view) *their decision-making* constantly reinforces the value set of the organisation (particularly around sustainability, inclusivity and trust) to an extent I have not previously witnessed in corporates! ... Second, the organisation recruits managers, franchisees and team-members on a 'people like us' basis... It has a very low staff turnover with volunteers returning year after year because they share a passion for what the YHA is trying to do: it holds real meaning for them! ... Third, the language and behaviours of the organisation constantly reinforce the values with 'gossiping success' stories opening every meeting and staff really trying to find positives about one another! ...

- **Outcomes** – the outcome of this approach is that the organisation is acutely aware of its priorities and where its 'true north' lies... this mobilises and controls behaviour in ways which are consistent with what the YHA is trying to achieve... Given the dispersed and idiosyncratic nature of the network, managing through policing/checking will not eliminate system breakdowns, particularly in relation to the safeguarding of young people... what the values do is provide a strong compass or code of conduct of the way in which people are expected to act... it sustains a quality product, providing a strong backstop to the policies and procedures already in place... It also means that the YHA continues to be a successful and relevant organisation, in spite of the competitive pressures it faces... Stakeholders (managers/franchisees, staff, customers, suppliers and external agencies) understand and appreciate its differentiated positioning and the contribution it is making... In fact, I would (humbly) venture to say that the YHA has probably been around and will endure longer than most of the companies profiled in your book... it's strong value set playing a large part in its long-term viability! ...

THREE KEY 'BINDING VALUES' FRANCHISOR QUESTIONS

1. Do you have an *inclusive* set of values that – in the absence of direct explicit instruction – will implicitly guide behaviours and *quality* choices on the front line?
2. Do your senior leaders live and act the values?
3. Do those who transgress – including high performers – feel the 'electricity of the organisation'?

CHAPTER SUMMARY

This chapter has considered how franchisors deliver their product and promise, binding their franchisees in by providing quality service support, timely information/data and a set of values that (in the absence of explicit instruction) shape intentional/purposeful behaviours. But what are we to make of the analysis and narrative above? What are the key determinants of franchisor success during the delivery process? Again, the text and case studies above point to specific transactional and relational exchange archetypes being deployed by winning franchisors to ensure favourable outcomes with their franchisees. From a **transactional** standpoint, 'support structure and services' (Musgrave) are particularly effective when '*experts*' design 'robust and top draw' systems (*services exchange*); 'financial control systems' (PSA Citroen) can be more effective when they 'pay out *incentives* to the best performers' (*monetary exchange*); and 'binding values' (YHA) provide a 'strong compass or code of conduct' which 'sustain a *quality* product' (*product exchange*). With regards to **relational** factors, 'support structures and services' (Musgrave) work well when the importance of 'localness' is *recognised*/encouraged for stakeholder 'attachment/engagement' purposes (love exchange); 'financial control systems' (PSA Citroen) succeed when they provided '*honest* and accurate real-time input and output data/information' (*information exchange*); and 'binding values' (YHA) are brought alive by *inclusive* 'non-hierarchical' behaviour by franchisor leadership groups (*status exchange*). However, important as delivery is, how do franchisors ensure that they keep up with market trends and stay abreast of competitors? The next chapter will examine how successful franchisors develop their brand over time to sustain its relevance and success.

DEVELOP

The third significant activity that franchisors should undertake – beyond designing and delivering – is relentless development of the concept and product. This is where things become problematic. Many texts on franchising provide excellent hints and tips as to how to set up and run a franchise but – possibly due to a lack of insight or empirical research – they provide scant advice regarding transformational/incremental development. It is also true that many 'early years' franchisors pay insufficient attention to this area, being mainly concerned with rolling out their original concept; profit growth being derived from system rather than 'same store' organic growth. Clearly this is unsustainable! If franchisors are concerned purely with driving the network to drive fee revenue – without paying due attention to developing the margin/profit of stores within the system – ultimately they will face relationship and trust breakdowns. In addition – in mature networks – if they appear to be focused upon on 'extracting rents' from existing sites to grow their share of the 'profit pool' – without introducing any *novel* initiatives to grow their franchisees' businesses – they will undoubtedly encounter major issues. So what do successful franchisors do in this area? First, they are adept at initiating, leading and implementing *top-down transformational* initiatives. Second, successful franchisors are highly competent at managing *field-based operational process improvement*; and finally, they are extremely effective at encouraging *middle-up-down knowledge transfer* which leads to added-value outcomes.

TRANSFORMING OPERATIONS

When franchisors launch a concept into the market (either 'greenfield' or conversion from owned/managed) it is highly probable that – if it is initially successful – they have exploited a white space in the serviceable market that had been hitherto ignored/overlooked by potential competitors. In their dash for spatial pre-emption, franchisors will concentrate on achieving network primacy quickly. There comes a stage, however, when 'second movers' enter the fray with concepts that – through a process of enhancement (technological, product/supply chain, facilities and service delivery concept) – start to erode 'first mover' competitive advantage. Indeed, macro forces such as the economic environment, globalisation, regulatory intervention, unremitting digital development, changing composition of the external labour market and consumer expectations for quality and affordability have inevitably increased the pace at which franchisors must evolve their product in order to maintain efficiency and competitiveness.

In response to these challenges, many *mature* networks have had to embark on transformational change programmes promulgated by existing or, more likely, new management, with numerous goals including: behavioural modification, new technology/machinery or work-practice implementation. However, the process of conceiving and implementing change in franchise systems is ridden with problems, not least the levels of resistance and inertia due to the *perceived franchisee costs* (financial contributions and time/effort). Franchises have generally grown through being successful in addressing markets in *specific* ways in the past. The strategy, structure and processes of the network are supported by a *cognitive bias* and *mental inertia* symbolised by a misguided belief that the 'way in which we do things around here' has been successful in the past and so will inevitably be effective in the future! There are also vested interests in maintaining stability: franchisees have insufficient skills and capabilities to do what is required in the new world. Where their power, status or influence (particularly amongst multiples) is likely to be undermined or threatened by change they are apt to fall back on the previous structure/contract in order to protect their position. Other reasons for resistance include positive rhetoric being juxtaposed against disruptive/chaotic reality, restrictions in freedom/autonomy and fears that destabilisation will bring costs such as reduced incentives/increased sanctions. A natural consequence of these countervailing forces to change is that franchisors believe that they are left with little choice other than 'change the franchisees' in order to enact their transformational agenda.

However, in a franchised context – unlike a standard 'managed' organisational context – it is completely unrealistic for franchisors to assume that they can drive through aggressive change using a 'root and branch' clear out. Although, in theory, franchisors can apply the 'letter' of their contracts with franchisees which stipulate that they are empowered 'mid-term' to make (legitimate) changes to fee structures and/or the Operations Manual, legal challenges regarding 'restrictions', 'unfairness' and 'unreasonableness' can be made by disgruntled partners. Also, where do they procure a new stock of able/willing franchisees given the onerous circumstances that have led to 'vacancies' and the scarcity (due to capital, attitude and aptitude) of prospective substitutes? More likely, successful franchisors – alongside 'managed churn' of the network' – seek to co-opt franchisees in more elegant ways to accept radical change. But what are the *qualifiers* and *differentiators* for driving through transformational development in a franchised network?

Principal qualifiers for success in this area are the existence of *'democratic governance'/participative communication* structures that enable franchisors to gauge franchisee *readiness*, enable them to *address mindsets*, *sell benefits* and then *implement* change.

- **Participative/democratic structures** – as a precursor to effecting successful transformational development it is vital that franchisors have a mix of formal/informal communications/consultation/information channels in place that help them to 'animate' the network over proposed developments:
  - *Consultative* – although it is not mandatory for franchisors to have consultative mechanisms in place, many quasi 'codes of practice' would advocate it as 'best practice'. Types of consultative mechanism include:
    - Associations – a recognised franchisee association with elected representatives that represent the collective views of the network to 'management'
    - Advisory councils/committees – a set of bodies (operating in conjunction with, or independently from, the association) that preside over certain functions/processes such as marketing, operations/services and/or supply chain
    - Voluntary groups – ad hoc joint-party groups that are formed for particular initiatives (product, pricing and/or technology enhancements).
  - *Information/communication*:
    - Meetings/conferences – cascaded meetings (national, regional and district) that provide information updates and an opportunity for feedback

- Digital/telephone platforms – instant information channels that allow franchisors to address *immediate* concerns
- Newsletters – weekly/monthly round-ups of latest/ proposed developments.

- **Assess readiness** – a major benefit of having all/most of the channels listed above is that the franchisor can gauge receptiveness and readiness to any major development activity. Generally, the readiness of franchisees will be contingent upon factors such as:
  - *Lifecycle positioning* – whether franchisees are 'early-compliant', 'mid-challenging' or 'mature-accepting', which will dictate morale/ psychological preparedness
  - *Previous experience of change* – previous experiences that have been positive or negative will shape outcome expectations
  - *Absorptive capacity* – the capacity of franchisees (in terms of resources and capability) will also affect abilities to absorb major changes.

- **Address mindsets** – having assessed readiness, franchisors must 'work the channels' by 'resetting' any negative mindsets through the following methods/messages: *'burning platform'* ('call to arms' refreshment/change message), *flattery* (reinforce sense of contribution and importance), *capacity* (create 'room' through task allocation – see below) and *'telegraphing consequences'* ('warn' wilful saboteurs and blockers).

- **Sell benefits –** hypothetically, the changes that are afoot have been piloted (often in stores proximal to HQ) and have demonstrated real benefits that do not smack of pure self-interested opportunism on the part of the franchisor! This being the case, franchisors must 'sell-not-tell' through their channels – taking on-board insights/comments to make conciliatory modifications which demonstrate that they are listening. When selling the benefits, successful franchisors will highlight and provide:
  - *The benefits equation* – B minus $C = PFO$ (benefits – costs = positive franchisee outcomes). In the process of constructing this equation, franchisors should avoid giving 'overblown' benefits statements (so-called 'polishing the turd') by presenting a realistic summation of benefits (i.e. efficiency) and personal/business costs (i.e. time, effort and capital).

- *'Unlearning' time* – a promise of sufficient time and space to 'learn' and 'unlearn' without any detrimental consequences (i.e. penalties or sanctions).

- **Implement** – once the transformational activity is 'sold in', the franchisor might use joint co-ordinating committees to oversee implementation. From a managerial perspective, it also important that they have sufficient 'change capability' to ensure they 'land' things effectively. Thus, guiding 'change leaders' on the franchisor side will need the following skills: ability to manage conflict, strong interpersonal skills, project management capability, high levels of leadership/flexibility, capacity to manage processes and a mindset that moves beyond managing the change curve (i.e. franchisor change leaders should seek to 'be ahead' of the game, not only anticipating and embracing change but also actively engaged in framing change policies of the future).

But what are the winning *differentiators* for franchisors enacting transformational development/change?

- **Separating content/process** – empirical evidence demonstrates that whilst trialling the *content* of major changes is ideally suited to a franchised system (due its risk-taking profile), it is more effective – once proof of concept has been established – to pilot the *process* of its roll-out/implementation within an 'owned'/managed context (Sorenson and Sorenson 2001). Thus, where organisations have 'split' estates, judiciously using one side (franchised) as an 'innovation incubator' whilst using the other (owned) as an 'implementation design platform' affords the greatest prospect of long-term success.

- **Co-opting 'big dogs'** – in addition, the success of major change programmes rests not just in getting the 'selling right' to the whole network but through ensuring that key opinion formers (such as large successful multiple franchisees) 'come out' in favour first. How is this achieved? *Recognising* their skills/status and pandering to their egos by including them in the trials helps, as does a promise (tacit or explicit) that they will be the first 'recipients' of the changes.

- **Transformation *and* continuity** – franchisors must be careful, whilst making radical transformational changes to their concept/business model in response to external 'macro' forces, that they do not throw the baby out with the bathwater. That is to say, they would be wise to preserve/protect the 'true north' (purpose) and/ or values of the concept. In fact, weaving these binding norms/ beliefs into the narrative surrounding the changes can only strengthen franchisor claims that the transformation is intended to be sustainable and mutually beneficial. Throughout the change, franchisors must also pay due attention to the (benefi-cial) financial outcomes/*incentives* for franchisees to maintain buy-in (see the following case study).

Case Study 8 – Transforming Operations at Domino's Pizza Group

Patricia Thomas is an industry-leading franchise consultant, having previously been Director of International Development and Executive Director of Operations of Domino's Pizza Group (DPG) UK. Previously, she held senior positions with Domino's (US) following stints at the Michel's Baguette French Bakery Café franchise and Houlihan's Restaurants.

When I joined DPG UK as Executive Operations Director in 2006 I identified two major objectives: to transform the *quality* and *speed* of operational execution in our store network. Due to the growth surge of the brand, it was acknowledged that our operational team had 'fallen behind' in ensuring that the basics were done brilliantly – certainly our franchisees lacked a degree of faith and buy-in to what they were trying to achieve… standards and systems adher-ence were perceived by some as unnecessary effort and cost… lip service was paid to enforcing standards and OM breaches were not uncommon. However, the one major attribute that DPG had was a fantastic culture that had been fostered by the CEO and his team – a healthy paranoia about keeping ahead of the competi-tion… a hunger and real desire to anticipate or fix 'chinks in the armour' that might prove costly in market-share terms in the long run… this applied particularly to network growth, product develop-ment and marketing… But how did I galvanise our operations team

CONTINUED …

and franchisees to transform quality and speed at the store level? … when I reflect back, it was through creating *strong relationships* and a strong sense of *mutual self-interest* (what was good for us as a franchisor was also good for them as a franchisee!)… This is how I went about it…

Coming into the role, I decided that I would spend the first 100 days visiting 100 stores to 'watch and listen'… this period allowed me to acquaint myself with the operations team who accompanied me to their stores and to 'touch' over 50 of the 150 franchisees we had at that time… This was in addition to the 'day job' – administrative duties, meetings, budgets, staffing, marketing etc. didn't stop for me to do this! … It became clear to me that the operations team required 'redirecting' and that our franchisees needed to under-stand why operational excellence was important to their bottom line… I started to work on our relationships with our franchisees by having informal meals and drinks with many of them, 'bringing them back into balance' (overcoming objections and problem raising) by recognising their contribution… asking about *how* they had got here today – listening to their stories, which almost served as a conscious reminder to them *why* what they were doing was important… We also set up regular calendar communications events which were designed to inform franchisees honestly and directly what we were doing, seeking their buy-in to changes… The message that I conveyed relentlessly during these interactions was that we had to get better at executing the brand… I used my experiences in the US as a powerful anecdote to highlight how operations that lose focus on product quality and speed of delivery can 'drift off'… but what I also did was to demonstrate empirically a financial link between investing in staff training, deployment and equipment, their positive effects upon operational execution and customer satisfac-tion/sales out-turns. I used 'live' examples of operators that had good Operational Evaluation Reviews (OER) and speed-of-delivery scores that had translated into great sales figures (this had never been done before)… showing that investing in your business really pays off! To ensure constancy of purpose, we also tied OERs and delivery times into specific targets with related 'rewards and

CONTINUED …

consequences'... At the same time the company introduced 'real time' comparative (store vs store) delivery data that showed up on FOH EPOS systems at store level and invested heavily in digital ordering systems... the cost for which was shared between the company and the franchisees...

The net impact of all these changes was a dramatic improvement in operational execution... OER scores moved from 3.53 stars on a 5-star scale to 4.27 stars – the highest achievement of any market in the Domino system. During this period of time, average sales per unit grew by 47% and the number of stores in the UK and Ireland grew by 62%... but – as I said – the way we drove these changes was by improving fundamentally our relationships with our franchisees; not through formal committees (where members can sometimes be driving their own agendas) – but by one-to-one, face-to-face communications where we got the message over... reminding franchisees about the 'why', selling the financial benefits of 'doing it right' and providing extra data/support to make it happen... One further thought I would add is that, given the transitory nature of much franchisor management, it is important that operational transformation is led by leaders with credibility who really *monitor 'the incentive to perform' and care about franchisee profit*... winning franchisors make 'good' sustainable profit rather than 'bad' short-termist gains! ...

THREE KEY 'TRANSFORMING OPERATIONS' FRANCHISOR QUESTIONS

1. Have you ensured that the financial *benefits* of transformational change outweigh its *costs'* implications for franchisees?

2. Have you communicated the over-riding *incentive* for change effectively – especially with the 'big dog' opinion formers in the network? (Either through formal democratic structures or informal social means.)

3. During the process of change, have you preserved the base essence/values of the brand (for continuity purposes)?

IMPROVING OPERATIONAL PROCESSES

Whilst centrally led transformational change programmes and/or top-down initiatives are vitally important, the franchisor must also facilitate/encourage operational process improvement (OPI) (usually through field-based personnel) which will not only increase their network resilience but provide perceived value-added benefits to SUFs and MUFs (Edger 2012, 2013). Why are OPI skills such an important aspect of the franchisor's support package? First, in spite of trying to achieve locational uniformity, every site in the network will have nuanced differences. Due to footprint constraints (imposed by landlords and/or legacy real estate) and locational differentials that impinge upon the rhythm of the business (i.e. demographic profile, high street versus mall etc.), field-based personnel have ample opportunity to advise/coach improvements to the FOH process flows and local marketing/promotions of each site. Second, operational execution will vary throughout the network meaning that the field has ample opportunity (within a set framework) to make *value-added* enhancements to BOH processes that will improve levels of operational excellence. But what are the qualifiers and differentiators for effecting continuous improvement at unit level?

As regards qualifiers, what the field should seek to do, when assessing 'micro' improvements, is *to understand* what an operational process is and relentlessly seek site-based improvements that reduce costs/increase sales whilst driving perceptions of speed, quality and dependability:

- **Understand OPI principles** – in his seminal book, Ray Kroc describes how he believed it was important that field-based personnel had 'formal operations lessons' in areas such as customer order fulfilment and food production processes (1997: 125). Certainly, McDonald's were pioneers in transferring insights from synchronised manufacturing into service environments and a prime example of an organisation that still today believes strongly in the principles of 'operational and process improvement' (OPI). It is therefore vital that field-based operatives understand the *definition* of a process – *the movement of product/ingredients, customers and information from one stage to another where added-value activities occur* – alongside *objectives*, '*shapers*' and desired *outcomes*:

- **Objectives** – good processes have the following attributes: 'lowest' cost, 'highest' sales, speed, dependability, flexibility, safety and quality.
- **'Shapers'** – good processes require constant investment in 'enablers' such as *staff*, *technology*, *facilities* and *machinery*.
- **Desired outcomes** –
  - *Throughputs/Rhythm* – removing pinchpoints and barriers and/or improving machinery/technology/staff capability will increase throughputs 'rhythm of the business'.
  - *Dependability* – reducing the number of process stages and decision points theoretically increases quality/dependability by limiting operator error.
  - *Capacity Utilisation* – good processes maximise capacity through rapid customer 'turn' (i.e. customer order fulfilment) and 'day part' fulfilment.
  - *Costs/Sales Relationship* – input reductions (i.e. staff costs/effort) married to simultaneous and output optimisation (i.e. sales and productivity) are a key outcome of operational process improvements.
- **Improving operational processes** – previous sections referred to the ways that franchisors seek to monitor/control their franchisees through FCS (auditing, measurement and correction) and through instilling a 'binding values' system. Such activities are designed to provide franchisors with 'outcome assurance' but – as stated above – not every business is exactly the same and 'micro' operational development/improvements can yield positive results. But what do the best field-based personnel do?
  - *Analyse/observe* – gather quantitative data (see 'Franchisor Control Systems' in Chapter 3) and watch operations/customer behaviour 'in the field':
    - *Location* – How good is this location? How visible is it? What is its footfall/traffic/competition? How can we attract more attention?
    - *Car parking* – What is the car parking capacity? How safe and secure is it? Is it used solely by our customers?
    - *Layout* – What is the size and layout of the unit? What are the FOH and BOH blockages?

- *Service cycle* – What is the customer journey from entry (digital/physical) to exit? How smooth is the experience? What are the *functional* blockages?

- *Experience* – What senses are stimulated positively by the visit? How effective are the *emotional* stimulants?

- *Product and promotion* – Does the range address the local market? Are the promotional mechanics fit for purpose?

- **Plan** – formally discuss (possibly in business strategy meetings) findings/insights with the franchisee or his/her nominated representative and agree a 'joint' plan for remedial action (training, marketing, machinery, facilities and/or technology enhancements). Delineate central support/field/franchisee 'by whom, by when' responsibilities.

- **Do** – implement the action plan, ensuring that assigned franchisor responsibilities are executed as agreed (promissory speed).

- **Review/reward** – regularly monitor (sanction adjustments?) and *recognise* added-value performance.

- **Embed** – incorporate improved process as a BAU (business as usual) activity.

- **Rollout/diffuse** – if the process improvement has a generic application, rollout across the portfolio (see 'Knowledge Transfer' below).

- **Isolate/tolerate failure** – if operational process 'enhancements' fail, accept the cost and move on.

But what are the differentiators for successfully executing operational process improvements at site level within a franchised network:

- **'Seeing the differences'** – as previously discussed, franchisors who permit a 'circle of compromise' to operate with regards to FCS conformance – allowing deviation in extenuating circumstances – are far more likely succeed than their peers. Granting some latitude/'slack' is a useful means of generating mutuality and reciprocity. The same applies to operational processes. Whilst the field can assist/coach operational improvements that bring the franchisee in line with the Operations Manual, they perform a critical role in *seeing the differences* between sites. That is to say, they can spot the nuances and idiosyncrasies of their sites and (within reason) suggest operational improvements to franchisees that will result in high value-added outcomes. Thus – perhaps counterintuitively in standardised franchised contexts – field-based operatives should not only be conditioned to enforce uniformity but have the intuitive judgement/wisdom to *facilitate local adaptation*.

- **Support response/flexibility** – one of the major problems that field-based personnel face in franchised organisations is a high degree of what might speciously be termed 'central inertia'. Often changes on the 'front line' happen rapidly and local responses are required urgently to counter competitive threats. Whilst effective field operatives can 'get things done' by networking and exchanging with central support staff, it is incumbent upon franchisors to create an *expert*, 'can do', imaginative, resourceful and flexible culture at head office. Often, the field will complain that the centre is 'behind the curve' and that they have to act outside of permitted rules/norms to satisfy operational demands. Thus, one of the main differentiating factors of successful franchisors is that they have support structures/services that have the *expertise*, licence and motivation to provide swift 'back up' to the field to improve operational processes.

Case Study 9 – Facilitating Constant Improvement at Dome Café (Australia)

Andrew Thomas is Operations Director for Dome Café, a thirty-year-old quality coffee and classic food brand that currently has 62 stores in Australia (a mixture of 12 'owned' and 50 franchised) with a further 50 in the Middle East and Southern Asia. An experienced hospitality operator, Andrew previously held senior operations roles in leading UK food and beverage companies.

...Dome Café is an extremely successful self-styled 'quality coffee & dependable' food concept that focuses upon 'strong all-day trade'... It has been built up patiently and evolved since inception over the past thirty years to a position where it is a highly sought after

CONTINUED ...

franchise in the Australian market (under the Australian franchising code of conduct, our managed stores provide ample empirical evidence of their trading success!) ... Up against some formidable local and international 'café' competition it has continued to develop its positioning (it started life as high-end 'artisan European'), with 'classic' food now constituting 70% of its trading mix (up from 30% 15 years ago)... New stores have 200 covers and are designed to cater for 'all needs' both in terms of customer profile (business, family, groups etc.) and occasion/'daypart' (breakfast, 'mid-morning coffee', lunch, 'afternoon coffee & cake', 'dinner & socialising')... The turnovers and EBITDA of the new stores are industry leading... Franchisees (who pay a Aust$125k franchise fee, 65k development fee, 6% royalty fee, 2% advertising and promotion fee and are tied to proprietorial coffee-bean purchases) can generate impressive ROIs on agreements that run on 10–5–5 or 10–10 terms... Many of our original franchisees are still with us – and in numerous instances own up to three or four cafes...

One of the main things that differentiates us from our competition is our operating philosophy... We want our franchisees to run businesses that are high on 'emotional connection' with their local customer base... loving and recognising their local communities – acting in a democratic way; respecting diversity... providing places of 'comfort & welcome'... This means that – from an operational point of view – we empower our franchisees to understand local needs and flex the guest experience using products and services as props for interaction in a bid to exceed the guests expectations... although we have a fixed framework in the business (specified design, standards and core product), we are quite open about what our franchisees are 'free to do' (in a spirit of 'purposeful autonomy')... we apply less of a top-down approach – we trust our franchisees to do what is best for our customers at any given occasion... To this end we have an extremely 'lean' support centre (only 20 staff with high levels of functional expertise – particularly our food-safety consultant) and continuous improvement in the brand is very much driven through 'co-creation and collaboration' between our domain experts and franchisees... a sort of 'user-centred design' approach... Rather than 'over-managing' the sites... making franchisees too reliant on

CONTINUED ...

expert field support... we are strong advocates of 'peer-to-peer' and 'competence-to-competence' skills development and knowledge transfer, and have deployed online platforms to support this approach... Three areas highlight how our operating philosophy is brought to life:

- **'Surprise-to-delight' service** – ...rather than imposing a rigid chain-of-service, we encourage self-expression and ingenuity... for instance, if two businessmen are having an intense discussion over coffee, taking over two glasses of filtered water from the condiments station moves customers perception from (what we term) 'surprise to delight!' ... in order to make this happen we encourage recruiting for 'will rather than skill!' ...

- **Interactive idea swapping** – ...we encourage our franchisees and their managers/staff to share ideas over the interactive on-line platform Yammer... this has proved particularly useful for 'idea swapping' around growing top-line sales at key seasonal events (Mother's Day this year was one of the biggest trading days in our history), community initiatives, events and evening time-slot 'filling' ('show-and-tell' events, jazz sessions etc.)...

- **Self-governing standards** – ...we don't have an army of 'checkers' and 'policemen' – we operate in a 'spirit of trust' with our franchisees... Yes, we have defined standards (specified in the OM) and have food-safety reviews (regularly conducted by an external agency) but we use digital technology to monitor displays, cleanliness, cook-offs etc. ... We keep our franchise fees down (they haven't changed since at least 2001!) by operating a 'lean' support structure – we expect our franchisees to reciprocate by being responsible and professional... After all, they've ploughed money into the business – why would they jeopardise their livelihoods by 'breaching' through sloppy standards?! ...

Overall, Dome has very good relations with its franchisees which are, first, grounded in the continuing success of the brand (which is financially beneficial to both parties)... second, we believe in 'listen and understand' rather than 'tell and do'... third, we are patiently evolutionary rather than revolutionary (important if you are promoting

CONTINUED ...

local autonomous behaviour)… fourth, we are believers in communicating honestly with our franchisees; setting unwaveringly high
standards and expectations that our franchisees both understand
and buy into…

THREE KEY 'CONSTANT IMPROVEMENT' FRANCHISOR QUESTIONS

1. How equipped are your field-based support staff 'to see the differences'?
2. Have you got appropriate franchisee 'peer-to-peer' and 'competency-to-competency' processes/forums in place?
3. Have you defined areas (outside the main framework of the brand) where franchisees can exert 'purposeful autonomy'?

KNOWLEDGE TRANSFER

Where do the ideas come from for transformation/improvement and how can they be diffused more effectively across the franchised organisation? In the sections 'Transforming Operations' and 'Improving Operational Processes', above, it was implied that transformation is conceived, tested and spread top-down, whilst improvement occurs at a 'micro-site' level. This is a simplistic analysis. Successful franchisors develop their concept relentlessly through harvesting/transferring ideas from every source available: externally through competitor analysis and internally through effective knowledge-transfer processes. Empirical research has demonstrated consistently that SUFs and IMFs are highly effective at innovating within local markets due to their proximity, whilst MUFs are very competent at improving operational execution by virtue of the fact that they have their own field-based structures (Garg 2013). Innovation, improvement and invention can be found throughout the chain but systemising its transference – codifying *tacit* knowledge so that it can be diffused *explicitly* for the benefit of the network – is highly problematic. Previous reference has been made to issues such as obsessing with network roll-out at the cost of incremental organic development in order to drive revenues; but in the case of knowledge transference, several other issues impinge upon its dissemination and adoption. We need to understand both what these *barriers* are and the main solutions (both qualifiers and differentiators) that successful franchisors apply to overcome them.

- **Barriers to knowledge transference**
  - *Lack of trust* – a belief amongst innovators in the franchised enterprise that their ideas will be diluted/stopped due to 'non-conformance' or that they will be punished for deviation.
  - *Different cultures/languages/frames of reference* – inability to transfer ideas because of differing/resistant attitudes and 'sacred cow' protection.
  - *Lack of time* – distance and 'business as usual' (BAU) activities prevent transmission/adoption.
  - *Status/power* – franchisor management layers and complex structures prevent transference.
  - *Limited absorptive capacity* – personnel across the franchised entity do not have the capability (due to education, training and motivation) to absorb/understand ideas.
  - *Knowledge hoarding* – possessors of innovative knowledge/ideas guard them for reasons of 'internal competitive advantage' (due to the fact that franchisors set up their reporting systems to compare region vs region, district vs district, unit vs unit etc.).
  - *Error intolerance* – a belief by the generators of insights that if these fail to work, they will be blamed/punished for mistakes.
- **Solutions to blockages**
  - *Lack of trust* – face-to-face communications to build 'social capital' (national/regional/district meetings, conferences/exhibitions, training days, store visits etc.)
  - *Different cultures/languages/frames of reference* – education and rotation of franchised personnel (including job swaps, rotation, placements, short assignments, projects and working parties).
  - *Lack of time* – create time/space for franchised idea exchange and deploy smarter methods for communication (digital solutions: webinars, discussion forums, apps, e-newsletters etc.)
  - *Status/power* – collapse franchisor hierarchies (remove unnecessary layers and get technocracy/support 'closer' to

operators/franchisees) – make ideas more important than status!

- **Limited absorptive capacity** – educate both managers and franchisees for 'cognitive' flexibility ('think' not just 'do').

- **Knowledge hoarding** – reward/recognise the 'sellers' of knowledge within the system and encourage reciprocity between parties through incentives, awards and public recognition.

- **Error intolerance** – remove gameplay, blame, sanctions and retribution.

But what are the winning differentiators in stimulating knowledge transference across the network?

- **'Social loafing' elimination** – to ensure that any knowledge-transfer process is fair and equitable, franchisors must eliminate *social loafing* and *bystanding* by those franchisees who wish to *free ride* upon the efforts of others. In district meetings, for instance, there will be franchisees who willingly share their knowledge and insights in open discussion whilst others (for various reasons) will sit in torpid silence. How are they activated? Celebrating the success of those that contribute positively to the process – 'pour encourager les autres' – is one approach. More effective, in the case of penalising 'takers', is to put them at the bottom of the list in terms of support and new initiative roll-outs.

- **'Deeper'** *inclusivity* – much of the literature relating to franchising conceives of the key dynamic in the business model (due to contract and agency) as being the franchisor–franchisee axis. Very little is said or understood about the contribution that the front-line employees of franchisees make in improving/developing the product. Successful franchisors go beyond just creating/sustaining relationships with their franchisees: they dig deeper within the organisation to create bonds with the visible representatives of their brand. In the case of knowledge capture/transference, they value and reward the insight/contributions of their franchisees' staff not only because they are useful in developing the brand but also, crucially, these members of the system might one day be franchisees themselves!

- **Support function 'sharing'** – in addition to encouraging the transfusion of knowledge across the network, successful franchisors also foster effective information exchange and sharing within/across functions (see Case Study 10 below) to improve/enhance product *quality*. Although this is relatively easy to achieve in national contexts – where support staff are (generally) based out of one head-office location – matters are complicated across global structures. Obvious solutions include structural design and reporting lines – although encouraging cross-company project/working-party participation and/ or collaboration, which enables staff to build strong ties and contacts, is generally far more effective.

Case Study 10 – Sharing Best Practice in Häagen Dazs International

Clive Chesser was International Operations Manager for Häagen Dazs (owned by General Mills), responsible for the operations of 680 café stores in 56 countries: one-third company owned, two-thirds run by joint ventures, master and individual franchisees. Here he recalls the process of designing, piloting, capturing best-practice process/content insights and rolling out an international branded service experience.

...It had become clear to us that the in-store Häagen Dazs 'brand service experience' (BSE) was not delivering the emotional connection that befitted a quality product positioned around 'indulgence': there was a mismatch between what the brand stood for in grocery channels and what consumers said that they experienced in our store cafes. In many ways, it was worse in mature brand lifecycle markets (such as France, Spain, UK and US) than elsewhere, although developing markets required attention due to cultural issues... What did I do? ... *First*, I constructed a major stakeholder map comprising internal (Regional VPs, Store Directors, support functions: HR and Marketing) and external stakeholders (master/individual franchisees, joint venture partners). Then I went out around the world and sold the project... There was more resistance to the idea of revamping

CONTINUED ...

service in markets such as China (positional power factors) and France (brand life cycle) where, culturally, they were not necessarily attuned to the benefits of such a project. In Japan I needed 'four yeses' before I got a real yes! *Third*, having got broad support and money we engaged consultants and really dug deep to under-stand the customer journey and the various service touch points. *Fourth*, we constructed a model for a pilot in four territories: this comprised a completely new service concept 'bringing the brand to life' backed up by intensive interactive training programmes that were adapted to local nuances (although the overall measures for the pilot – sales, customer loyalty, customer satisfaction – were the same for all). *Fifth*, we trained out the new 12-step programme with desired behaviours in a 'train the trainer' fashion – top to bottom. So… making people feel welcome, bringing the brand to life through offering free samples, demonstrating product knowledge, identi-fying needs, speedy service, fun check backs etc.

Although the line were absolutely critical in helping us land this project (for example, in Spain – which accounted for 10% of the estate – the Store Director was totally enlightened and on-board) support was patchy at first. One crucial enabler to the success of the whole project were the Regional Training Directors (particularly the three 'bright and progressive' RTDs representing Latin America, Latin Europe and Southern Asia). Prior to this project, these RTDs had not really interacted on an international basis (global HR being run on a devolved Regional basis) but this project brought them together. We held a number of formal and informal meetings/calls either as a group or individually… As the project progressed they were able to share insights and best practice both in relation to which 'product systems' were working in certain markets and also how best to co-opt the operational line (upselling commercial/performance benefits)… In addition, they were pivotal in mobilising their field-based trainers who interacted with local operators/fran-chisees to ensure materials reflected both the central principles of the BSE and customised local needs/preference… Language was important… although I was fairly relaxed about local 'iterations', I was reliant on the global training team to ensure a combination of a high degree of consistency together with 'inclusive interpretation'

CONTINUED …

for local cultural 'fit' (my Mandarin, for instance, isn't very good!)...

Overall, the pilot was a huge success with sales increasing by 13% and loyal customers (those likely to repurchase and recommend) increasing from 30% to 43%. Another consultancy, engaged purely to measure outputs, also reported very positive variances on ROI, other customer satisfaction indices, employee engagement and retention. During roll-out, the success of the new service concept continued. Each training and implementation package was customised for each local market (what was permissible in Saudi Arabia, for instance, was different to what was permissible in Brazil). However, the customer measures remained the same across the world, allowing like-for-like-comparisons. I believe the best practice and insights shared amongst the RTDs and their teams were crucial to this project's success... Also, where the Store Directors were either culturally or personally tuned into the programme (often through RTD influence), it was a major success as they influenced their franchisees or store managers positively. As a major transformational change programme, the role of the RTDs in capturing, sharing and training out best practice both in *process* and *content* terms, through their close liaison with field operations, was pivotal...

THREE KEY 'KNOWLEDGE TRANSFER' FRANCHISOR QUESTIONS

1. Does insightful knowledge/intelligence flow within/across support functions or is it 'hoarded'?
2. Where blockages occur, what are the main reasons – cultural, ideological or temporal?
3. How do you stimulate a 'learning culture' across the franchise system exemplified by the circulation of free-flowing knowledge and expertise?

CHAPTER SUMMARY

This chapter has considered how franchisors successfully develop their brands by enacting 'macro' transformational change, encouraging 'micro' process improvement and facilitating knowledge transfer within/between functions. Constant development and refreshment is critical for brand progress in a fast-changing competitive context. Indeed, ensuring that they have a 'learning culture' to combat commercial threats/challenges cannot be the subject of choice for franchisors – it is a matter of necessity!

But how do franchisors co-opt both their staff and franchisees in developing the offer? Again, dominant themes and insights emerge from the text and case studies above, which continue the insights of the previous chapters. Brand development is facilitated by transactional and relational exchange archetypes under the aegis of mutuality and reciprocity. From a **transactional** standpoint, 'macro' top-down 'operational transformation' (Domino's) succeeds when it 'is led by leaders... who really monitor the "*incentive* to perform" and care about franchisee profit' (*monetary exchange*); 'improving operational processes' (Dome Café) involves a high degree of 'user-based design', 'peer-to-peer' and 'competence-to-competence' development facilitated by 'staff with high levels of functional *expertise*' (*services exchange*); and 'knowledge transfer' is eased by an environment where '*quality*-based products' are a given (*product/goods exchange*). From a **relational** perspective, 'transforming operations' (Domino's) is helped by 'bringing (franchisees) back into balance' by '*recognising* their contribution' and 'listening to their stories' (love relations); 'improving operational processes' (Dome Café) is assisted by fostering a climate of 'communicating *honestly*' with franchisees (*information exchange*); and 'knowledge transfer' involves '*inclusive* interpretation' for local cultural fit (status exchange).

Having examined how franchisors win, this book will now turn its attention to how the other party in the relationship – the franchisee – succeeds.

HOW FRANCHISEES WIN

The previous three chapters provided grounded insights into how franchisors might go about designing, delivering and developing a successful and sustainable (retail) business format franchise proposition. What emerged from both the analysis and the case-study narratives, summarised at the end of each chapter, was the importance – in addition to transaction mechanisms – of franchisors exercising high levels of social exchange (both transactional and relational) to foster mutuality and reciprocity. Thus, to explain successful relations between both parties taking a purely economic view (through agency and contract) as some commentators do (Rubin 1978, Combs and Ketchen 1999) is clearly wrong. But these chapters relating to franchisor success factors are an incomplete summary of what constitutes a successful franchising model. What about the franchisee perspective? How do they ensure not only that they become a vital cog within a winning formula but also that they contribute to its long-term viability and success? This section will address these questions by outlining – on the basis of contemporary experience and research – how franchisees win through, first, *engaging* with the franchised business model/brand, second, *executing* the concept either as a single, multiple or master franchisee and, last, contributing to the *evolution* of the product through influencing, bargaining and (in some cases) deviant behaviour!

ENGAGE

As a starting point, the first thing that successful franchisees do is to *engage* psychologically with both the content and process of franchising. They manifest this behaviour at three levels. First, they buy into/demonstrate a positive pre-disposition to franchising through possessing a franchised mindset. Second, they 'fit' with the concept, displaying some form of emotional attachment – essential if they are to become raving advocates of the brand to multiple stakeholders (backers, staff and customers). Third, they engage effectively with the business planning process, ensuring that – at a local market level – they are 'set up for success'. In contrast, unsuccessful franchisees display opposite behaviours – they lack a 'franchisee ethic' to establish energetically a small business, many fail to identify/connect with the core product/brand and some fail to formulate professionally and systematically a realistic business plan with appropriate tolerances (accounting for both an upside and a downside). How franchisees display a positive *franchised mindset*, *brand/concept suitability* and form *effective business plans* will now be considered in turn.

FRANCHISED MINDSET

Anybody considering becoming a franchisee must ask themselves whether or not they have the right psychological profile or mindset to embark on such an undertaking. Although franchising offers a more structured way of 'working for yourself' in an environment that (when it works!) provides a safer, more supportive and enduring way of establishing a business, it still requires a high degree of personal effort and commitment to succeed.

Common problems arise when aspirant franchisees approach franchising with the misguided attitude that it provides a 'softer' life-style option than being a salaried 'wage slave': it does not. New entrants into the industry frequently remark that they had severely underestimated how hard the initial phases of establishing their franchised business would be – in spite of all the back-up and support offered by the effective franchisors discussed in the previous chapters. Also, issues arise when franchisees who have a deluded conception of themselves as innovative entrepreneurs are confronted with the constraints of a standardised offer in what might be termed the '**franchise paradox'**. Virgin franchisees who believe that buying into a franchised system will afford them *unfettered* autonomy (as opposed to *structured* independence) are likely to become highly disappointed and frustrated.

If new recruits go into the franchised business model with the right attitude and mindset, they are much more likely to be successful. They are less likely to suffer from the severest forms of lifecycle transitioning (particularly the early 'needy' and mid-cycle 'rebellious' phases) and will be able to handle the multiple ambiguities and complexities of being in an inter-firm relationship in which they have limited room for manoeuvre. But what are the qualifiers for success in this area?

- **Positive motives** – franchising is not an option for people who think it is an 'easier' or instantly more lucrative job than being a salaried employee. Buying and running a franchise is an exhausting and exacting process for newcomers and (in many instances) provides poor absolute returns during the first few years. Whilst the potential benefits of buying a 'good' franchise include better assuredness/security of business success by being part of a well-crafted and well-tested brand/system, it is not a 'soft' pathway to *quick* or massive enrichment. Research has consistently demonstrated that successful franchisees are realistic; rapid financial gain is not their main guiding motive for accessing this form of business model. Rather, successful franchisees tend to be hardworking 'grounded aspirants': first, valuing the independence that franchising offers compared to employed status; and second, being motivated by the prospect that the fruits of their labours *might* (in time) lead to financial gain.

- **Appropriate profile** – in addition to identifying the right motives, franchisors and academics have isolated a number of key personality factors common amongst successful franchisees that provide a useful template against which those wishing to 'sign up' can calibrate themselves:

- *Agreeable* – as franchisees have to co-exist with a powerful partner (in the form of the franchisor and their agents) the ability to foster good relations through being – in most instances – co-operative as opposed to confrontational is an essential trait. Indeed, extreme extraversion and ego-driven behaviours on the part of the franchisee are likely to result in conflict and a breakdown in relations over the longer term according to a major study by Morrison, who concluded that 'franchisees higher in agreeableness and lower in extraversion are more likely to develop congenial relations with their franchisors'. (1997: 39)

- *Emotionally stable* – in addition to agreeability, franchisees require high levels of emotional control with which to sustain consensuality. As things rarely run smoothly in any franchise – malfunctions occurring across a range activities from time-to-time – franchisees require the ability to 'bite their lip' and focus upon controlling the controllables within their business(es) rather than wasting emotional energy by 'losing it' with their franchisor. In addition, rather than constantly trying to challenge the status quo and adopting a 'glass half empty' mentality:

  > emotionally stable franchisees are [more] likely to follow system directives, facilitate cooperative working environments and ultimately develop enduring relationships with their franchisors. In comparison, highly extraverted franchisees are less likely to accept the franchisor's dominant power position within the network, which may impede the development of strong and stable franchising relationships…

  > (Dant et al. 2013: 291)

- *Conscientious* – the third characteristic required by franchisees is a high degree of conscientiousness, often termed the 'franchisee ethic'. What does this mean? In part, it implies forensic application of the blueprint and an absence of (excessively) opportunistic behaviours – but it also refers to possession of a hard-working, grafting mentality. Yes, successful franchisees must follow diligently (most) rules/procedures so as not to fall foul of the system or the law, but they also require a high level of energy or 'installed capacity' to work. Franchising is no place for slackers, shirkers or malingerers (or for creatives or intellectuals).

- **'*Entrepreneurial*'** – to a large extent, 'franchising [can be defined] as a form of cooperative relationship among entrepreneurs' (Gassenheimer et al. 1996: 68). Thus, what great franchisees (especially MUFs) require, alongside the mix of fairly (conformant) characteristics detailed above, are selective *facets* of entrepreneurial behaviour such as: optimism, drive, risk, flexibility/agility and courage. That is to say, they shouldn't be entrepreneurial in the sense that they seek wholesale changes to the system per se; rather, they have the attitude of mind that, firstly, leads them to choose franchising, secondly, exploit their local opportunities and, thirdly – as Chapter 7 will demonstrate – contribute to developing/ extending the system over time *co-operatively*. Successful franchisees manage/exploit the conundrum of being a business, within an inter-firm framework governed by a senior partner, by maintaining a 'controlled' entrepreneurial disposition.

- **Realistic expectations** – it is natural within human nature – and certainly during the process of choosing to go down the franchising route (where a blinding sense of 'escalating momentum' can occur) – for people to latch onto positives, regardless of obvious negatives. The problem of 'cognitive bias' – making one's mind up before all the facts are widely considered – which leads to 'mental inertia' and resistance when reality dawns is an ever-present danger within franchising. Virgin franchisees might have high expectations regarding its potential returns (based on overblown stories of success either by 'boastful' franchisees or 'exuberant' franchisors) which are seriously disappointed by their initial experiences. This poses major dangers, best overcome if franchisees – in addition to examining the efficacy of franchising itself – also rigorously examine brand/concept suitability and formulate a proper business plan (see 'Concept/Brand Suitability' and 'Business Planning' below). Hence, a *sense of realism, perspective and proportionality* is required for anybody taking the franchised route, to enable them to cope with (inevitable) set-backs and challenges. Such a mindset will result in higher satisfaction, better relations and greater longevity within the business:

  > Although franchisees possess non-experiential expectations regarding the future performance of their franchise unit and system, they are only able to measure these against ongoing assessments of how effectively their franchisor delivers on the

'promise' of the franchising business model... on the assumption that equitable (or even proximally equitable) relationships are sought, we suggest that subsequent perceptions of equity and fairness in the franchise relationship will inform a franchisee's (dis)confirmation of (normative) expectations and impact the relational character (and functioning) of future franchising exchanges...

(Grace et al. 2013: 220)

If there are some fairly universal qualifiers for franchisee success in the area of mindset adjustment, what are the attributes that really stand out as differentiators?

- **Resilience** – the point made about emotional stability, above, requires extending. In addition to high levels of self-control, franchisees require extraordinary levels of mental (and physical) toughness. Mistakes and missteps will be made by both the franchisee and (at times) the franchisor and the staff the franchisee employs. It is the ability of the franchisee to cope with these challenges with calmness and equanimity whilst maintaining a fierce resolve that marks the winners out from the losers. Using stressors as a motivation rather than debilitating blockers – feeding off the obstacles to be overcome rather than being stalled by them – is a key requirement. It should come as little surprise that some of the most successful franchisees in the developed world over the past thirty years have been 'developing nation' immigrants who have deployed 'sweat equity' (both physical and monetary) to establish thriving franchised businesses. Possessing an extraordinary work ethic, a strong business mindset, *respect* for authority and high aspiration (bolstered by the lack of opportunity in 'traditionally minded' corporates), they are prepared to 'go the extra mile'. Their hardiness in the face of adversity (and willingness to *collaborate* in tight social groups) has made them ideal franchisees, something that indigenous recruits have (in some cases) clearly lacked.
- **'Extended' mindsets** – the concept of appropriate mindsets requires extending beyond just the franchisee her-/himself. It is important that all those within the franchisee's orbit – not least the franchisee's family – buy into the venture in this domain. The franchisee's family and friends form important support systems that provide reassurance, guidance and support. For instance, in

the early days of set-up, the franchisee's partner might continue working in a full-time job to provide a source of income until the breakeven point is reached. The physical/financial sacrifices required in establishing a franchised business are enormous – all affected parties (in addition to the franchisee) must display similar levels of conviction/belief to get them through the 'grind'!

Case Study 11 – Successful 'Member' Profiles in Symbol Convenience

Jerry Marwood is the MD of Blakemore Spar Trade Partners. Blakemore Spar is an extremely successful part-owner of the convenience retailer, Spar UK, supplying and operating approximately 300 managed and 700 'member' (franchised) outlets in the Midlands, Wales and London. Previously, Jerry held senior positions in 'big box' food retail, national consortia and symbol organisations.

... Symbol convenience retailing in the UK has a lighter controlling framework than 'tight' brands such as Costa or Starbucks... Being less prescriptive, many 'symbols' rely on attracting more entre-preneurial/ innovative types of 'members' to deliver their system against standardised multiple convenience competitors (the likes of Tesco, Sainsbury's and Asda)... At Spar we operate a light franchising *'guild member'* model of association... To provide a context, I will firstly outline what this model is and then, secondly – given its specific idiosyncrasies and requirements – outline what I believe are the *key characteristics* of successful 'members' of our system:

- **'Guild member model'** – Spar is an international phenomenon (its largest business is in South Africa and its fastest-growing one is based in China) that was a first mover in retail convenience in the UK nearly sixty years ago! ... In the UK, it is a huge buying consortia that distributes goods under the Spar banner... It is split into five geographical areas with different 'master' compa-nies (Blakemore being the largest) that directly manage and co-opt 'members' into regional guilds... To become a member

CONTINUED ...

of the guild you have – in exchange for a weekly fee and modest investment in the fascia/fit out – to agree to buy through the Spar network, to adhere to minimum operational standards and to implement seasonal marketing plans… In Blakemore, our 700 'member' network is divided between SUFs (large-volume single stores passed down the generations), 'Spar-focused' MUFs (SUFs growing to multiple scale), 'Portfolio' MUFs (multiple stores owned by 'portfolio' business people) and 'Corporate' MUFs (corporates that run Spar formats as adjuncts to their primary businesses)… Our points of difference in our model are:

- *80/20 buying flexibility* – … unlike 'hard franchised' retail (where only 2–3% of goods can be bought from outside the system), 'members' can buy up to 20% of their goods outside the system…

- *Localisation/customisation* – … this buying flexibility allows our members to be extremely agile at a local level… fighting against the 'big boys' purely on price and range is not an option… Rather, 'members' are actively encouraged to find points of difference through customising their offer to the local market… connecting with local communities… To this extent, our support system expertise is (in comparison to our competitors) extremely consumer (rather than customer) focused…

- *Collaboration* – … the guild system (arranged on district, regional and national levels) is an extremely collaborative and co-operative arrangement built around respectful rela-tions… we pride ourselves on encouraging 'peer-to-peer' idea sharing OR 'crowd sourcing' for ideas…

- **'Ideal member profile'** – … given the challenging competitive landscape and operational model, what do successful 'members' (franchisees) look like? … Obviously, different 'member' segments require different competencies with large SUFs needing a 'hands-on' management style whilst MUFs require good BOH systems/processes allied to great FOH coaching mechanisms… But overall the generic requirements include:

  - *Conformity* – … product ordering adherence, minimum standards maintenance and marketing execution…

CONTINUED …

- *Creativity* – … local entrepreneurialism… a creative spark for the 'selling' experience… imagination to 'see the differences' in order to exploit the opportunity…
- *Conviction* – … the ability to trial, test and see things through… to keep going when others might give up or question 'why'! … 'Members' who get what we are trying to do and are in it for the long term…
- *Competitiveness* – … to enjoy being the best… wanting to win awards and receive industry/peer recognition… a burning desire to be the best…
- *Collaborative mindset* – … the ability to share ideas with peers/support services and participate in open feedback channels…

So the context (both industry and firm) inevitably shapes the type of 'members' (franchisees) that – to my mind – are successful… I would add – and your readers will find this rather obvious (or disconcerting!) – the attributes that make certain 'members' successful are somewhat '*schizophrenic*!'… conformity is juxtaposed with creativity; competitiveness with collaboration! … The best seem able to 'jog and chew gum' – they know it is not an 'either/or' choice – success rests on making mature choices at the right time, in the best interests of the wider organisation and consumer! …

THREE KEY 'MINDSET' FRANCHISEE QUESTIONS

1. Do you have a resilient 'get back up and go again' mentality?
2. Are you capable of 'jogging and chewing gum' – *complying* with the brand standards whilst simultaneously showing 'local' *creativity*/ingenuity?
3. Do you have a confrontational or *collaborative* personality? (The latter being preferable in a 'mutually' beneficial business relationship.)

CONCEPT/BRAND SUITABILITY

Having the right mindset is the necessary precursor to entering franchising but what concept/brand should the prospective franchisee choose? In essence, this comes down to appropriate levels of match, 'fit' and suitability. Not only should the brand and the franchising type (mobile/fixed and/or service/business format) appeal strongly to the aspirant franchisee but (s)he must have the appropriate technical skills and/or developmental capacity to optimise its operation. In a format franchising, the business of running a retail store requires specific competencies, not least the requirement to lead and manage service providers. Generally, problems arise for franchisees with regards to suitability on three counts. First, they lack any real connection with the franchise beyond the obvious point that it is a franchise rather than a salaried job. Second, connectedly, some franchisees – due to their over-exuberance, highlighted above – fail to calibrate the brand's suitability through conducting a rational due-diligence process that analyses all the tangible (observable) and intangible (unobservable) aspects of the concept. Third, they lack the required behavioural (service and leadership) and cognitive (financial acuity) skills, allied to a lack of access to sufficient funds to set-up and run resource-hungry enterprises.

What criteria should franchisees use when searching for a brand that matches their aspirations/capabilities and how do they go about the search? Many 'how to' guides outline in detail the franchise process (Internet franchise portal search, brochure request, initial expression of interest, telephone interview, first/second meeting, returnable/non-returnable deposit, sign-up or drop out etc.) but what are the main qualifiers and differentiators in ensuring suitability?

- **Emotional connection** – successful franchisees are willing brand ambassadors who, by implication, have wholeheartedly identified/bonded with the concept. This occurs on two levels: an emotional connection with what the brand stands for and the nature of the work itself.
  - *Meaning/values* – franchisees are more likely to prosper if they connect to why the brand exists (as in meaning) and how it conducts its business (values and ethics). In the former case – the 'why' or meaning – if the franchisee believes that what they are doing constitutes some form of 'worthwhile' work, with likeable people with whom they strike up some form chemistry, they are inevitably going to be more motivated

through good times and bad. Often the culture of the brand will be reflected in the way they are processed/treated initially by franchisor representatives, which will give them some indication as to the integrity of the people they will be dealing with over the longer term. So to the latter point – the 'how' or values – whilst most franchisors will have 'values statements' (see 'Binding Values' in Chapter 3) prospective franchisees should think carefully whether the franchisor's actual values (exemplified through *demonstrated* behaviours) are aligned to their own code of ethics, fairness and propriety (see below). Before they sign up, good franchisees will ask themselves 'once the honeymoon is over, am I going to be treated as I would treat others myself?'

- ***Job satisfaction*** – academic studies on franchising constantly re-iterate the importance not just of personality/profile as a contingent variable affecting franchisee success but also the vital importance – given the arduous nature of the endeavour – of a high level of job satisfaction. That is not to say that prospective franchisees should select a franchised product that is associated with their previous employment (unless they have been corporate members of staff in the brand beforehand) or that they should actively choose something wildly unfamiliar. The point is that, given the demands of the role, franchisees should choose a concept whose functions/tasks seem vicariously interesting (making it easier to learn and operate). Often, franchisees only gain insight into what the role entails at the training/immersion stage of the process, once they have signed up! One way of mitigating this risk is to request taster days (before signing on) or to complete voluntary shifts for a 'helpful' franchisee to gain a better insight up front as to whether or not the nature of the work appeals. Should it do so, it is more likely that the franchisee will be happier; resulting in better performance, higher organisational commitment, more co-operative franchisor relations and a longer intention to remain. For instance, Morrison's (1997) study of 307 franchisees across four industries found that:

  > The average franchisee in this sample spent a tremendous amount of time at work (over 50 hours per week) and by virtue of their financial investment and contractual obligations to their franchisors [have to] demonstrate a strong commitment to their

occupation. Thus, the job satisfaction they derive from their occupation appears to have a relatively strong influence on outcomes [organisational commitment, franchisor relations and intention to remain]… [Thus we] found support for a relatively large correlation between job satisfaction and performance…

(Morrison 1997: 55, 58)

- **Proper due diligence** – aside from ensuring that they have a strong emotional connection with the brand and its nature of work, franchisees need to establish suitability by conducting *thorough* due diligence. Sometimes franchisees can get carried away by the (positive) promotional material they read on websites and in brochures, which present a one-sided view of the brand (upwards revenue forecasts, grand promises of support and 'halo' case studies of success). Faced with 'information asym- metry' (an incomplete knowledge of all the facts), potential franchisees can make some disastrous errors of judgement. It is as well to remember that essentially franchisors have a product to sell that generates them revenue – they are hardly going to (publicly) list the detractors of the brand. As a counterbalance, in the US franchisors are legally obliged to produce an FDD (Full Disclosure Document) that provides in-depth information regarding performance, litigation, network turnover etc. In the UK, no such obligation exists although some (ethical) franchisors will outline pitfalls and challenges to aspirants during one-to- one conversations/interviews; but this still depends upon the prospective applicant digging deeper by *asking the right ques- tions* to gain a fuller picture of the organisation and the concept. Chapter 2 outlined how franchisors construct their product and provides some guidance as to what successful franchised offers should look like; but what are the key questions that franchisees should ask during the 'courtship' phase of the relationship?
  - *Concept sustainability* – (*for start-ups*) what returns are you (the franchisor) making from initial sites? How is the serviceable market responding to the product (time, season, promotion, category etc.)? What is your pipeline and network plan (cluster or scatter)? What is your performance against 'similar' concepts? (*for mature networks*) What is the average store's sales trend over the past 3–5 years? What is your level of franchisee turnover (and is it going up)? Why do fran- chisees fail? Please give me examples.

- **_Fees/income_** – what percentage of income do you (the franchisor) generate from same store sales (and is it going up or down)? What are the worst store net profits? Why? After paying ongoing fees, how much net profit can I expect to make over a five-year horizon? What effect has product inflation had on average franchisee margins and pricing/turnover over the past three years? What incentives (fee breaks, free equipment, marketing funds etc.) do you offer new franchisees?

- **_Obligations/rights_** – for what reasons do you terminate contracts? Give me examples. How easy is it to exit the franchise if things don't go to plan? Give me examples. Are you a member of the BFA and/or do you subscribe to their code of conduct (how – give me examples)? In what areas am I free to exercise discretion?

- **_Services/support_** – aside from listed services (business planning, site finding, new store openings, operational evaluations, training, marketing, purchasing, menu management etc.), what do you mean by 'other ongoing services'? What is the structure of your support infrastructure? What level of staff turnover do you have at the centre and in the field? What is the average length of territory tenure amongst your Franchise Support Managers? Do you conduct 'internal service' surveys amongst your franchisees – how does it rate relations, responsiveness and effectiveness (which is the best/worst performing function – why)? Describe your formal communication/consultation channels? Give me examples of positive contributions.

- **_Territory/growth opportunities_** – under what circumstances do you reduce territory sizes? Please give me examples. Do your anti-encroachment clauses exclude other brand formats (i.e. managed, in-store concessions, mobile etc.)? (_virgin territories_) Why will this territory work? (_mature/re-sales_) Why did the previous franchisee exit? (_multiple growth_) How did your current MUFs build their chain within your chain?

- **Behavioural/financial capability** – business format franchises are people/resource intensive. The questions that prospective franchisees must ask themselves are whether or not they have the capability (existing or developable) to lead a team and manage finances in addition to having access to sufficient capital during early start-up phases:

- *Service leadership* – fixed retail formats provide a range of goods and services which involve multiple customer transactions. These transactions can vary in their frequency and intensity (according to time, promotion and season). Front-line service providers are the face of the brand and must deliver knowledgably and enthusiastically the concept's sequence of service to generate repeat business and positive advocacy. Thus, franchisees must have the necessary capabilities to manage and lead teams to meet customer needs, ensuring the right people are deployed at the right station with the right skills at the right time. The 'Single Unit Franchisee' section of Chapter 6 will expand upon how franchisees should develop, motivate and incentivise their teams optimise performance. Suffice to say that retail franchises are 'people businesses' and franchisees must have good organisational and motivational skills. For some aspirant franchisees, this is difficult either due to a lack of previous man-management experience and/or ingrained cultural biases (tendencies towards self-protective leadership and a master–servant mindset). These issues can be overcome if individuals have the capacity to either 'learn' new skills and/or 'unlearn' bad practices.

- *Financial acumen* – in addition to good leadership skills, franchisees need a high degree of financial acumen. What does this mean? Success or failure for the franchisee rests upon their ability to get the 'gearing' of their business right. That is to say they need to drive revenue and convert it into profit by *accounting* for fixed and *controlling* variable costs. To this extent franchisees must be able to 'read' their P&Ls understanding dependencies, linkages and connections between the numbers. Most franchisors agree that some of their best franchisees are their most 'financially literate' members of their network.

- *Capital resources* – finally, the franchising dream will fail to lift off if prospective franchisees have insufficient funds to buy the franchise and/or cash reserves to 'cushion' the first few years of trading. Business format franchises are cash hungry and most banks/lenders require least a minimum 30% cash contribution to a franchise purchase. With stretched resources, new franchisees might enter the system with limited working capital – a big problem if things start badly.

Franchisees must therefore make contingencies not only for buying the franchise but also for sufficient cover for 'early trading'.

If the points above give some clues to franchisees as to how they can assess brand/concept suitability, what are the differentiators that result in satisfactory matching?

- **Learning capacity** – the truth is that prospective franchisees will never achieve a 100% fit with a brand. Whilst they will cover some of the bases in terms of prior knowledge/skills, they will have gaps in certain areas. What is most important – if the brand passes muster in terms of interest, attractiveness and affordability – is that prospective franchisees have the cognitive capacity, 'open-mindedness' and *commitment* to learn. Conscientious franchisees who are willing to *commit* themselves to acquiring new skills stand a better chance of success than those that assume – due to the franchise's relative simplicity – that they can employ others to 'understand the detail to *comply*' once they have bought and set up the franchise.

- **Adaptability** – in addition, franchisees must accept that, as the franchised product changes over time, they must be prepared to grow and adapt with the concept/brand themselves. What they are purchasing today is likely to evolve in response to competitive pressure/customer requirements and they need to retain a flexible mindset, being prepared actively to contribute to improving the concept as it moves forward (see Chapter 7).

Case Study 12 – Mindset and Brand-Fit: The Franchisee View at GlobalBrand

Adrian Rhodes, an independent management consultant and researcher, worked with 'GlobalBrand' (a sector-leading multinational managed/franchised food service business) on four projects: new franchisee recruitment, franchisee management information requirements, store management success factors and national franchise consultation structures.

CONTINUED ...

In order to refresh its search and recruitment criteria, GlobalBrand and one of its incumbent suppliers asked me to establish – through empirical research – what the key characteristics of their successful franchisees were. How did I approach this? An obvious way would have been to harvest the views of franchisor management... but the recruitment/selection instruments were already reflective of their perceptions/prejudices! Actually, I did something counter-intuitive... What I did through both qualitative (one-to-one in-depth interviews and focus groups) and quantitative (a cross-franchisee survey) research was to ask franchisees within the network *themselves* what they thought the *critical behavioural dimensions* of successful franchisees were. This is what they thought the key success factors were:

- **Belief in the brand** – the first defining characteristic they came up with was utter commitment to, and belief in, the brand. What did this mean? Successful franchisees willingly bought into all aspects of the brand, namely: its identity, values, service delivery system, advertising/marketing mechanisms and massive commitment to training. Above all, they bought 'the system'.

- **Taking a long-term view** – the best franchisees realised that induction into the brand was (deliberately) arduous and that becoming a franchisee was, effectively, a life-style choice. The first few years would involve a 24/7 effort to get established... constant troubleshooting – dealing with detail all the time. ... Successful franchisees had metaphorically to 'live, eat and sleep' the brand to make a success of their businesses.

- **Realistic expectations** – in combination with the last point, successful franchisees understood from the beginning that franchising (even with this global powerhouse) was not a quick or easy route to instant fortune... they were realistic about initial income levels, profit margins and how much the company would 'take' from them... There would be no guarantee that after making a success of their first unit they would acquire other sites/territories within the system...

- **Detail and vigilance** – successful franchisees saw themselves as being disciplined – complying with and executing every single aspect of this famous brand: in the jargon of psychology, they

CONTINUED ...

had high levels of vigilance skills, relishing and being meticulous about product detail in order to protect the quality and reputation of the brand. It must be said that they were assisted in their task by GlobalBrand's excellent operational manuals which (for the purposes of their multi-ethnic workforce) were simple to read and digest... and it was typical of the franchisor that it asked me to *research* employee understanding of the training manuals and internal communications!

- **Entrepreneurism within a framework** – obviously successful franchisees followed the specified system and framework but they also described themselves as 'MDs of their territories'... they could make choices with regards to a host of operational issues... (in the case of MUFs) making quite significant media buying decisions...

- **People management skills** – successful franchisees identified this as one of the key characteristics, and observation of their relationships with staff showed it to be true. Great franchisees had the emotional intelligence and energy to manage effectively a wide range of people... they could get people to do what were intrinsically boring, moderately paid jobs but in their words 'get a buzz' going (through generating a sense of teamship – incentivising and recognising goal achievement)... They were astute in the hiring decisions – taking on 'cheerful staff' who gave great customer service in spite of some of the repetitive, messy jobs they were called on to do... 'enriching' mundane jobs through providing excellent training and progression opportunities... and they didn't just claim to have motivated staff: *research again confirmed it.*

- **Results orientated** – as this business was controlled/run through metrics (and lots of them), successful franchisees saw themselves as having good numbers skills allied to an obsession with *benchmarking.* Great franchisees (who generate healthy fee income) tended to be naturally competitive... in fact, many were frustrated that they did not get better information on how they were faring against their 'managed store' cousins! ...

During the course of my research I also explored the 'lifestyle characteristics' of successful (mainly male but also some female)

CONTINUED ...

franchisees, finding that: over 50% had an HND or degree; all had at least A levels; most were married home owners with a mortgage; they tended to read 'conservative' newspapers (the *Times*, *Telegraph* and *Daily Mail* rather than the tabloids); they had high levels of local community involvement, were previously employed in somewhat authoritarian organisations (the armed forces, the police, accountancy or the brand itself!) and were more interested in sport rather than creative pursuits. I concluded from this that successful franchisees tended to come from *'conformist'* rather than *'creative/ exploratory'* backgrounds – 'mild extroverts' who could get on with anybody whilst getting to grips with the numbers *and the details*! ...

THREE KEY 'FIT' FRANCHISEE QUESTIONS

1. Are you (or can you be) totally *committed* to contributing to the success and *growth* of this brand?
2. Do you have an infectious passion for *customer service* that will energise a 'front-line' team?
3. Have you got adequate *financial* and *numeracy* skills to interpret key data and plan/organise accordingly?

BUSINESS PLANNING

Previous sections have outlined how successful franchisees are properly engaged when they approach franchising with the right mindset and are suitably matched to an interesting and sustainable brand/concept. During the course of this bonding/attachment process, should the prospective franchisee wish to proceed with their interest in a particular site/area/territory, they must engage the franchisor actively with a robust business plan. This plan – usually formatted around templates provided by the franchisor or banker – should provide a detailed business case (years 1–2 monthly, years 3–5 annual) which addresses the scale of opportunity (location, demographics and competitive set), financial forecasts (P&L and break-even sensitivities), business builders (marketing and promotions) and other ad hoc considerations (local planning and employment sensitivities). Often franchisors will provide assistance and data to help frame this document or prospective franchisees will co-opt the services of a franchise consultant to help them construct a compelling plan. Common pitfalls in this process include the use of misleading/inaccurate data, financial forecasts that are gilded with optimism and insufficient detail relating to promotional/PR mechanics that will drive local traffic during 'slack' trading periods.

Given the necessity to get the franchisor and/or lenders to buy into their business plan so that they achieve sign-off to proceed, what are the key elements needed for inclusion in the report?

- **Location characteristics** – the franchisor will provide a template that will specify some (or all) of the following criteria with ideal numbers and characteristics: traffic flows/footfall counts, position/complementarity (urban, suburban, arterial and/or hub, centre, mall, park), 'generators' (residential, office workers, retail, leisure, other etc.), visibility, site access/travel lines, car parking access/capacity, public transport links, road network and facility size/dimensions. In reality, there will only be a couple of locations in the area that will be a similar match and these are most likely taken. The task for the franchisee is both quantitatively (with the assistance of professional consultants and/or the franchisor) and qualitatively (by observing site patterns) to propose the best available 'matched site' against the template.

- **Customer/demographics** – again, an 'ideal' market demographic will be provided by the franchisor against which the franchisee can measure site 'fit' including: 'ideal' total market size (within a specified travel time), age, average disposable income, number of households/families, % owner occupier, gender mix, religion and ethnicity. Local data for these areas can be drawn down from market information companies (either through consultant or franchisor services). What the prospective franchisee is trying to establish through this data is the viability of the store in a particular area by identifying *who* their local customers might be, *where* they are, *what* their habits/preferences are and *how* (s)he might reach them.

- **Competitive set** – another consideration is whether or not the franchisee is proposing to open a site in a saturated or 'lean' market. To this extent, (s)he needs to present a competitor ranking based on the following factors: proximity, positioning, product quality, amenity/environment, pricing/promotion and estimated sales. Included in this section should be the franchisee's ideas as to how (s)he can match/beat the strongest and defeat the weakest competitors! In addition, some consideration as to how one would counter potential entrants over the next five years (through a 'competitor intrusion plan') would also make a valuable addition to the report.

- **P&L and breakeven sensitivities** – having set out the market opportunity and competitive landscape the franchisee should provide a monthly P&L breakdown for the first two years (reflecting trading patterns and seasonal cycles), with years 3–5 scoped out on an annual basis. Again, 'best practice' templates will be provided by the franchisor and other sources such as banks and specialist franchised consultants which will help the franchisee build in the breakeven sensitivities created by the market data outlined above. This is a crucial part of the document that must be framed realistically with sensible ratios. The P&L outline should include: sales projections, variable costs, fixed costs and net profit (with their various sub-components). It should also go into great detail – after the 'headline' documents – to illustrate annual, monthly, weekly, daily and day-part estimated returns and breakeven points. Other factors such as average spend per head variances, the costs of mini-sparkle revamps and (in the case of multiple ambitions) the attributed costs to each site for multi-site overhead running costs should also be highlighted in this section of the report.

- **Local marketing/promotion** – a critical part of the plan will address how the franchisee intends to drive business during 'slack' periods (outside national/regional campaigns). To this end, (s)he should highlight mechanics that might be deployed at certain times (coupons, bundled offers and extra loyalty card points) alongside their appropriate channels (social media, apps, store website, targeted e-mail lists, local newspapers, posters, billboards etc.) combined with analytics that highlight start/ finish times/dates, breakeven elasticities, tracking mechanisms (redemptions vs sales generated) and post-promotion analysis methodology. The franchisee must also highlight local community activity and PR plans, demonstrating how they intend to connect/embed themselves into the fabric of the locale to increase trust and awareness.

- **Ad hoc considerations** – finally, other factors that might positively or negatively affect the business going forwards, such as competitor planning applications/consents, town/region retail/

residential strategies and large local employer plans, should be included.

Having presented a robust business plan, achieved agreement from the franchisor, funding from investors and the go-ahead from the lawyers, the franchisee will now be fully signed up. Start dates and training courses (classroom and on-site immersion) will be agreed and the identified premises will be procured/prepared. A full pre-launch programme (fit-out, recruitment, training, stocking, merchandising etc.) will be orchestrated by the franchisor and the franchisee will now prepare for opening!

The factors above are all 'hygiene' factors for a successful business plan – but what differentiates the best from the rest?

- **Heterogeneity as opportunity** – one thing that stands out from business plans that subsequently deliver is the fact that they don't just highlight symmetry with the brand templates but emphasise how they can overcome/leverage differences. It is highly unlikely that any proposed site will replicate exactly the 'ideal', so what successful franchisees do is recognise local nuances and *share* with the franchisor elegant solutions that might make these 'divergences from the mean' a virtue rather than a hindrance. In reality, the templates that the franchisor produces – whilst claiming empirical validity derived from 'best-practice' sites – are rarely perfect/accurate representations of the right location/market. Every franchisor has 'outlier' sites that do not fit the norm but are extremely successful – operator excellence often being cited as the key variable for 'out-performance'. Thus, prospective franchisees who make a powerful business case through seeing/addressing 'opportunistic differences' stand a reasonable chance of achieving sign off.

- **Rigorous scenario planning** – another aspect of successful plans is the degree to which franchisees build in upside/downside scenario planning. Understanding trading tolerances decreases risk and increases resilience for both parties. Posing a number of 'what if' scenarios and demonstrating that the business can *grow* – withstanding various shocks (aggressive competitor activity/encroachment, economic slowdown, product inflation, reputational damage, key staff poaching etc.) – only strengthens the franchisor's view that the prospective franchisee has thought through the sustainability of their business model and is a 'serious' business person who is likely to thrive.

Case Study 13 – Getting a Single Unit Franchise Business Plan Accepted by Domino's Pizza Group

Richard Johnson became a single-unit franchisee with Domino's in June 2009 and currently holds a multiple portfolio of four sites. Previously, Richard had a successful corporate career, rising to IT Director in his last company with executive responsibility for a team of 120 staff.

Below, Richard outlines his *motives* for becoming a franchisee, how he made his *franchise choice*, the *selection process* he went through, the *business plan* he put forward to panel for his first business, how he was *inducted* and his overall *reflections* regarding his franchised 'entry' journey.

- **Motivation** – ... having spent over twenty years in the corporate world, I had always been attracted by the notion of setting up my own business; indeed, I had already 'dabbled' by starting a number of little ventures... I was aware, however, that getting from '0–60' with a start-up business – which would provide me with the right income and lifestyle – would take time... As I wasn't the same age as Richard Branson when he started his empire (!), franchising seemed to 'fit the bill' of offering a proven business model... enabling me to 'hit the ground running' with an assured income stream...

- **Franchise Choice** – ... once I had made the decision to franchise, I had to decide which franchise worked for me... I attended franchise shows, read the magazines and researched franchised options on the Internet... It seemed to me that there were two sorts of franchises on offer: 'man with a van' or larger 'fixed' format businesses (which offered scale, but few seemed to be really successful!) ... Being ambitious, I was attracted to the latter category... I made a shortlist of targets based on *returns*, *growth potential* and the '*way in which they did business*' (rigid/standardised or flexible/autonomous)... In the end I ended up with a shortlist of one – Domino's! ...

- **Selection process** – ... I had actually met the Domino's people at a show and really liked them... I filled in the application form

CONTINUED ...

and sent it off... I was then given an intensive telephone interview... I was then invited to a face-to-face interview and then, finally, a panel interview where I presented my business plan for a prospective Domino's unit...

- **Business plan** – ... the business plan I put together with enormous amounts of information being provided by Domino's (template 'standard' sales, costs, location characteristics etc.) proved helpful for a plan that ultimately addressed two audiences: both the franchisor and the bank... My report addressed the site opportunity that Domino's had put to me and included the following sections: my profile/background, the business entity running the business, why I had chosen Domino's, short/medium/long-term targets, P&L/cash-flow forecasts (including breakeven sensitivities), background on store/area/competition, SWOT analysis on the store, marketing/growth plans, seasonality, staffing and overall financing... I think what might have impressed the panel was the 'local field' research I had conducted prior to putting the report together... I had spent a lot of time 'on the ground' looking at the competition (existing and forthcoming) and understanding the town (its development plans and demographics)... Of particular importance were the store-based marketing opportunities which I highlighted to raise awareness, traffic and penetration; *signage* at the rear of the premises next to a high-volume commuter train track, extended *opening hours*, meshing national and *local marketing* and significant *local community involvement* initiatives...

- **Induction** – ... my plan was accepted and – in a 'parallel' manner' whilst I bought the franchised business – I underwent a comprehensive month-long induction programme with Domino's which was excellent but demanding (they have a lot to tell you!): classroom learning by day and working in a store in the evenings... actually, this fitted really well together. From being accepted in April, I was trained and in place in the store by June! ...

- **Reflections** – ... when I look back, the process of doing a business plan was not just a 'tick box' exercise... It enabled me to think really deeply about the business and it really did act as a

CONTINUED ...

'reference' for me when I began to run the business... Make no mistake, running a franchise is really hard work – you really have to put in the hours to be successful... Sometimes you do not have 'downtime' really to think – but you do have a plan where (at a point in time) you had clearly 'marshalled' your thoughts for the future... To me it was a 'live' document, and when I look at the plan now [I can see that] it was a useful 'route map' and compass... indeed, we did deliver the plan for growth and hit the 'numbers' as expected – we did what we said we would do! – something that was well received by the franchisor... Of course, when you are in situ, loads of other ideas also provide added value. ... Today, I have four stores with an Ops Manager, bookkeeper, store GMs (with three assistants each) and nearly 120 team members... which, when I think about it, is the same number of people who used to work for me in my old corporate job! ...

THREE KEY 'BUSINESS PLANNING' FRANCHISEE QUESTIONS

1. Aside from the data provided by the franchisor, have you completed adequate 'local' field research to spot opportunities?

2. Is your *growth* plan realistic – does it include upside and down-side sensitivities? (Make sure the downside is 'covered off'.)

3. Are you prepared to implement the plan ruthlessly, consulting and updating/improving it as appropriate?

CHAPTER SUMMARY

This chapter has examined how successful franchisees engage with their brands through having the right mindset, the correct 'concept fit' and an appropriate business plan that acts as a blueprint for success. But what are we to make of the narrative and the case studies above? What are the essential factors that ensure franchisees prosper? What emerges from the texts and accounts is that franchisees – like franchisors – exchange a range of 'currencies' with their owners in order to forge excellent relation-ships. Furthermore, these exchange mechanisms mirror those deployed by franchisors, albeit that they are slightly nuanced and more 'subject specific'. Insights from the research data for this book suggest that successful franchisees also engage in **transactional** (*monetary, product/ goods and services*) and **relational** (*love, information and status*) **exchange** processes in order to generate reciprocity/high levels of assistance from the franchisor.

From a **transactional** point of view, winning franchisees possess the right 'mindset' (Spar) if they have a '*collaborative*' mentality 'to share ideas with peers/support services and participate in open feedback channels ' (*services exchange*); achieve 'concept/brand' (GlobalBrand) fit if – amongst other things – they are 'disciplined... *complying* with and executing the every single aspect of this famous brand... [with] high levels of vigilance skills... being meticulous about product detail in order to protect the quality and reputation of the brand' (*product/goods exchange*); and – with regards to 'business planning' (Domino's) – they 'deliver the *growth* plan' and 'hit the numbers as expected' in order to please the franchisor (*monetary exchange*). In terms of **relational** exchange, franchisee entry 'mindsets' (Spar) should be '*respectful*' towards franchisor staff and peers, particularly in highly 'co-operative' participation systems (*status exchange*); and their 'concept fit' (GlobalBrand) will be enhanced by 'utter *commit-ment* to, and belief in, the brand... (buying) into all aspects of the brand, namely: its identity, values, service delivery system' (*love exchange*) and 'business planning' (Domino's) focused on 'local field research' which – in addition to benefitting the store – *shares* important insights with the fran-chisor (*information exchange*). But having engaged with franchising, the brand and their local business how do they successfully execute the offer to the satisfaction of the franchisor?

EXECUTE

Following engagement and acceptance/induction into the system, the successful franchisee now concentrates all their efforts on executing the brand in their unit(s). The franchisee now has a number of obligations (detailed in Chapters 2 and 3) that (s)he has to fulfil – not least to run the brand to 'minimum operating requirements' and begin paying the franchisor for the privilege of being part of their network! Often franchisees – because they have been so wrapped up in the trials and tribulations of locating a franchise, accessing finance and legal support, finding a site, presenting a business plan, going through intensive training, supervising fit-out and pre-launch preparation – delude themselves that opening day is the end the process. It is not – the real race now begins! Whilst the franchisee will receive extensive support from the franchisor in the first couple of weeks after opening, contact will become more infrequent, mainly coalescing around structured visits, bouts of field training and business meetings one or two times a month. Therefore, it is largely up to the franchisee to deploy the skills/knowledge they have acquired during induction and through the guidance of the comprehensive Operations Manual to deliver a seamless and flawless product and service. How do they achieve this? The answer is that approaches to execution differ according to whether the franchisee is an SUF (single-unit franchisee), MUF (multiple-unit franchisee) or IMF (international master franchisee). These will be considered in turn below.

SINGLE UNIT FRANCHISEE (SUF)

SUFs are owner–managers who – due to low levels of managerial distance and a tight span of control – are able to exercise 'direct' daily on-site supervision. As the main conduit for franchisor interaction, (s)he should also (theoretically) be proficient at implementing central initiatives and, given personal proximity to the local market, be highly effective at addressing local needs/preferences (Garg 2013). The problems they generally encounter are temporal/resource related: in the early days in particular – whilst they are still learning 'on the job' with a lack of skilled on-site support – SUFs can struggle to meet the required brand standards. Problems are exacerbated if their business plan turns to dust in the 'white heat' of day-to-day operations, several factors having been misjudged or simply missed out! Rather than being opportunistic or resorting to 'shirking' (ignoring 'expensive' systems or cheating), this is when SUFs need to apply a rigorous approach to their operational execution – leaving no stone unturned in their pursuit of excellence. What the best do (within Operations Manual and best-business-practice parameters) is relentlessly concentrate upon executing the '3Ss' – systems, standards and service. The checklists below provide some insight into how the best organise, manage and lead their units.

- **Systems implementation**
  - *Labour processes*
    - *Labour ratio tracking* – ensure unit keeps to forecast and/ or budget/cash target.
    - *Rostering and deployment* – ensure that unit is fully manned to undertake duties required during peak and non-peak trading sessions. Check seasonal rostering plans; ensure sufficient labour capacity to service volume. Check 'right person, right place, right time'.
    - *Employment law compliance* – ensure that units are operating legally and in accordance with cultural/religious norms (i.e. following working-time rules, migrant diaspora workers have permits/passports, proper age, gender and diversity, regulatory/religious adherence etc.).
    - *Unions* – deal with local representatives of organised labour where necessary. Ensure good relations are sustained for operational efficiency purposes.
  - *Standard operating procedures*
    - *BOH Tasks* – ensure standard back-of-house task lists and section 'details' are adhered to (i.e. data uploads, delivery checks, storage, security etc.). Monitor food production procedural adherence within catering and dining contexts.

- *FOH Tasks* – monitor front-of-house tasks such as: pre-opening procedural adherence, 'daily duty manager' sweeps, section accounting, till procedures etc.

- **Availability, stock and waste processes**
  - *Availability* – ensure appropriate stockholding is in place to service demand. Monitor replenishment and check supply chain to ensure constant availability.
  - *'Must stock' items* – check that stock complies with OM purchasing obligations.
  - *Reconciliation* – ensure cash takings reconcile with sales and stock.
  - *Theft and shrinkage* – check security and surveillance processes to minimise pilfering, 'knock offs' and shrinkage.
  - *Waste* – monitor and minimise non-consumable *and* perishable waste.

- **Sales and promotional monitoring**
  - *Daily/weekly sales* – check daily and weekly sales against budget and last year.
  - *Day-part analysis* – monitor sales flows by timeslot; check throughputs and efficiency
  - *Promotional adherence* – ensure national and regional marketing plans are implemented (avoid 'free-riding').
  - *Pricing accuracy* – check coding exception reports; ensure pricing accuracy.
  - *Ad hoc discounting* – Check 'end of line'/'out of date' pricing and sales times (too early?)

- **Due diligence and essential maintenance processes**
  - *Safety* – check fire-safety compliance (testing, extinguishers etc.) and monitor on-site customer incident book.
  - *Hygiene* – check adherence to statutory and company procedures. Ensure food hygiene standards are compliant (i.e. one hundred percent food hygiene training for food handlers). Check pest and rodent control systems. All equipment maintained and serviced?
  - *Legal compliance* – 100% under-age alcohol sales training (in territories where legally permitted).

- *Hazards/breakdowns* – ensure all essential maintenance requests are actioned on time and to specification.

- **Ad hoc processes/change initiatives**
  - *Pre-opening* – oversee new opening processes; staffing, stocking, training, handover etc.
  - *Local suppliers* – maintain and monitor 'local suppliers' list (product and maintenance contractors).
  - *New product launches* – train and communicate new product launches.
  - *Change initiatives* – act as conduit for all new change initiatives (i.e. promotions, operational systems etc.).
  - *New site locations* – scan for new site opportunities.

- **Standards adherence**
  - **Merchandising and display**
    - *Planogram checks* – ensure merchandise is displayed according to specification (i.e. facings and perishable range display).
    - *Promotions* – check promotion materials (signage, posters, shelf pricing, gondola ends etc.).

  - **Store environment**
    - *Cleanliness* – check cleaning rota and cleanliness (especially toilets and trading areas). In addition, check external building/carpark, BOH stock rooms, staff changing and rest rooms etc. – the cleanliness of these areas will be linked to FOH standards!
    - *Sound, lighting and 'smell'* – ensure all 'sensory' sound, lighting and (where appropriate) 'smell' systems are functioning appropriately. Check speaker systems and background music loops, ensure the store is properly lit for security, safety and product-illumination purposes and check 'perfume' and ersatz 'odour' systems.
    - *Air conditioning and heating* – check functionality and effectiveness.
    - *Fixtures and fittings* – ensure fixtures and fitting are maintained and presented to the required standard.
    - *Store security* – check the robustness of the store security systems (both mechanical and human).

- *Local environment*
  - *External agencies* – fulfil a troubleshooting, problem resolution and 'relationship' role with local officials, authorities, landlords, environmental health, safety executives and external auditing agencies engaged by the organisation.
  - *Competitive scanning* – monitor local competitive activity. Respond (where permitted) and/or feedback to senior management or head office (if feedback loops in place).
  - *Social responsibility* – check links with local community (i.e. charities, fund raising, job schemes, perishable food distribution etc.).
  - *Local PR* – ensure unit has a high degree of local visibility through the local press.
- **Service-based sales drivers**
  - *'Local' HRM (human resource management)*
    - *Roles/responsibilities* – check that roles and responsibilities are clearly denominated, assigned and understood. In particular, ensure shift leaders have clearly specified pre- and in-session duties and tasks.
    - *Recruitment and selection* – appoint managers and assistants with appropriate behaviours and capabilities. Check store recruitment systems and hiring mechanisms to ensure 'meritocratic' attitudinal and skills testing.
    - *Communications/recognition* – ensure appropriate communications (weekly, daily and shift) are in place through the appropriate channels (face-to-face, intranet, e-mail, social media, notice/clipboard etc.) to disseminate key information, recognise outstanding performance and provide feedback.
    - *Coaching and training* – ensure that appropriate coaching and training mechanisms (in terms of operational requirements *and* culture/language) are in place and are being followed rigorously.
    - *Compensation/incentives* – check compensation/incentive levels against local market; ensure that sufficient talent is being attracted, retained and motivated.
    - *Performance appraisal* – ensure that regular team/staff appraisals are taking place to the required standards of development and performance metrics.

- *Store leadership* – check and audit staff satisfaction/ engagement, absence, grievance data etc.
- **Service concept adherence**
  - *Service flow* – ensure that customer 'touches' are applied in the appropriate manner (sympathetic to local cultural norms) at each stage of the service cycle.
- **Customer survey follow-up**
  - *Mystery customer* – monitor and action outputs from mystery-customer visits.
  - *Online surveys* – monitor and action outputs from online surveys.
  - *Web-based feedback* – regularly check and (where permitted) answer feedback on web-based forums and channels.
- **Service promise and complaints resolution**
  - *Service promise* – check that the service promise (i.e. no quibble return) is fulfilled – particularly in relation to 'click and collect' services.
  - *Complaints* – ensure that complaints are answered and rectified both in-store and at head office in accordance with company procedure.

Needless to say, the franchise control systems (FCS) and corporate infrastructure outlined in Chapter 3 will provide blueprints for the SUF to expedite most of the activities above. But what are the real differentiators for outstanding SUF operational execution?

- **Diagnostic capability** – as was highlighted in 'Franchisor Control Systems' in Chapter 3, although the sequence of under-standing, implementing, monitoring and correcting/*complying* is vitally important to deliver desired operational outcomes, it is the capacity to make linkages between interdependent factors (either enhancing/degrading operations) within the business's 'black box' that marks out truly successful franchisees. Knowing what 'input' operational factor affects certain customer/sales 'outcomes' is a vital cognitive requirement for effective opera-tors. For instance, if customer feedback indicates that service operatives lack 'product knowledge', some staff have been insuf-ficiently trained (possibly due to high turnover), are potentially 'bad selections' or are for various reasons demotivated (poor shift leadership and/or a lack of incentives, perhaps). Effective SUFs will make the right connections (through quantitative and qualitative analysis) and resolve the issues fast!

- **Support relations** – rather than seeing the 'centre' as an inconvenience to be circumnavigated, effective SUFs create very good relationships with both head office and field-based personnel with whom they *share*/swap information and ideas. By exuding agreeableness and emotional self-control (see the 'Franchised Mindset' section of Chapter 5) – rather than arrogance or resentment – successful SUFs get more out of the system than others, including better operational support.

- **Team purpose and values** – perhaps the most important thing that great SUFs do, however, is create aligned purpose and values amongst their unit team. SUFs – whatever they might think – cannot execute the brand single-handedly. Great SUFs are team builders who motivate and *share* information. They lead and inspire strong teams that know *why* they are there, *what* they are supposed to do and *how* they are going to do it. This enables the SUF to take time off and replenish their energy reserves, knowing that operations will run smoothly in their absence – the true sign of a great operation. It also enables them to build human capacity for expansion into multiple sites (see below) if and when the opportunity presents itself.

Case Study 14 – Achieving Single Unit Franchise Operational Excellence at GlassesInc

John Brighthouse is joint owner of a franchise with GlassesInc. One of the most successful optician chains in the UK, GlassesInc has prospered through funding its growth through co-opting joint venture partners that are attracted by its innovative business model.

The company that my business partner and I bought into has – I believe – a fairly unique business model that both reduces the risk and optimises the reward for all parties. My business partner is a

CONTINUED ...

trained optometrist and I am a retailer by background so we have complementary skill sets – I do the day-to-day business planning and FOH running of the unit and my partner handles the BOH technical 'lab' and 'professional dispense' side. The way the arrangement works with GlassesInc is that we agree to abide by their 'system' (brand, purchasing and service/standards) and they provide us with great national marketing (we pay about 6–8% revenue fee for this) and superb back-up (start-up, business planning, accounting, legal, marketing, IT, merchandising, buying, training operations and HRM advice etc.). The business was so successful from the off (we had one store in x for eight years; we have recently got another store) but it was bloody hard work... we worked flat out – me getting the FOH standards right whilst my partner (as I pull his leg) 'ground glass' all day! But how did we achieve the operational excellence that has eventually led to us being offered the recent opportunity?

- **Compliance** – I have to say the first thing we tried to do was what we called 'follow the brand givens'... We knew we had been fortunate to get accepted into a system that was spectacularly successful (financially)... there were certain mandatory givens in this brand (patient care, hygiene, legals, duty of care etc.) combined with a necessity to buy 'nominated' (quality) products and contribute to marketing... Our audit scores have always been excellent...

- **Local** – local knowledge counts for a lot in this brand – 'what is the demographic' is a major question (ages and incomes have a big effect in this business!)... What does the local customer need – what will our ordering patterns be... what new products will appeal to the local market?

- **Openness** – we also have – from day one – been totally open and *honest* about the financials... From my previous background, I know that our owner doesn't want surprises in terms of falling ordering patterns, late fees etc. ... We've never hidden anything – the company have been a great help giving us constant advice/input along the way...

- **Sharing** – this is a really great enterprise where we – as partners – really feel valued and part of something special... The fact that the founders are still in charge after all this time and many

CONTINUED ...

of the support staff have been here for 10, 20 years in some cases gives us confidence that sharing information with others is in our best interest... we get lots of ideas back... Yes, I meet other operators at regular meetings... but I know a lot of them individually now and we regularly share local knowledge that might benefit ourselves and the wider network...

Overall, my advice to any (retail) SUF that wants to succeed is, first, pick the right franchise, ... second, pick the right business partner... third, be prepared to work harder than you've ever done before... fourth, get great staff that can shoulder some of the burden (and pay them well!)... and fifth, never – EVER – compromise on your standards...

THREE KEY 'SUF' FRANCHISEE QUESTIONS

1. Do you understand how to *comply* with the key 'givens' of the brand (systems, standards and service) for the purposes of network consistency?
2. Have you got the right team in place at the right time to service customer needs?
3. Are you properly exploiting your *local* serviceable market (*sharing* your approaches and insights with peers and support services)?

MULTIPLE UNIT FRANCHISEE (MUF)

Having achieved operational excellence in a single site, franchisees can apply to exercise their 'rights to grow' and gain sign-off from the franchisor to acquire new units that will be run by their own managers. Academics have observed that franchisors are keen to promote this growth pattern because it reduces their monitoring costs through optimising good operators; reduces opportunistic/'shirking' behaviour, due to high incentives to perform; and when done well, accelerates network coverage.

[M]ulti-unit franchisees are better motivated to reduce the **monitoring costs** [of franchisors]... franchisors prefer MUF as compared to SUF to reduce the risk of **free-riding** at the local outlets... the franchisee's quasi-rents based on higher outlet-specific investments thereby increases the **self-enforcing range** of the franchise contract… [As] the self-enforcing range is higher under MUF compared to SUF, the **opportunism** risk is lower, and the franchisor less frequently uses disciplinary measures (litigation and termination) for contract enforcement. Consequently, a MUF reduces the **hold-up risk** due to the stronger incentive effort compared to a SUF. Furthermore, MUF systems have a relative advantage over SUF systems under the resource scarcity view… the use of a MUF increases the **organisational capabilities** such as monitoring, knowledge transfer and innovation capabilities and, consequently, strengthens the competitive position of the system. System uniformity, system-wide adaptations and system corporatization are examples of the organizational capabilities…

(Hussain and Windsberger 2011: 103)

Likewise, there are great benefits for franchisees transitioning from SUF to MUF status in a 'good' brand not least because it dramatically increases their earning potential, with many MUFs becoming multi-millionaires in their own right in successful franchises such as McDonald's, KFC and Dunkin' Donuts. Nevertheless, growing from a single site is fraught with issues, not least from people and financial perspectives. Franchisees must be careful that in moving people across sites to fill positions they do not 'hollow out' their capability in their original ventures, threatening the whole viability of their endeavour. Also, growth is expensive with costly pre-opening requirements (legals, business plan, property acquisition, design and fit out, recruitment/training, marketing and PR) and sufficient working capital for the start-up trading. Some operators can fund expansion through reserves but more often they will require loans or cash injections from new or existing partners/investors which increase ownership complexity. Other issues relate to distance and the fact that, as MUFs grow, they become more detached from their local markets and customers:

MUF-systems have lower [local] market capabilities compared to SUF-systems, due to SUF's higher degree of local responsiveness…

(Bradach 1995: 66)

In addition, bad site selections can result in MUFs spending inordinate amounts of time 'fixing' bad units, diluting their focus and returns elsewhere. MUFs can also be impeded by failing to develop the necessary skills/infrastructure to 'manage remotely'. But how do successful MUFs overcome these issues to execute the brand effectively? The answer is that MUFs need to address different things at various growth stages (up to 3 units, 4–9 and 10+) if they are to succeed:

- **MUF (2–3 units)** – in the early phases of growth MUFs commonly act like they did as SUFs, trying to run each site as if they were the manager! At this stage – when they cannot afford a multi-site support infrastructure – they need to disseminate their SUF systems, standards and service capabilities (see the previous section, 'Single Unit Franchisee') through leading/coaching their managers, developing capability so that they can spread respon-sibility and delegate certain tasks. Essentially, successful MUFs with two-to-three units achieve operational excellence without exercising direct daily supervision through monetary (good pay, conditions and incentives) and non-monetary (coaching, training, progression, communication, recognition etc.) exchanges. This frees up capacity for them to work 'on' rather than 'in' the busi-ness: improving marketing, finding great sites etc. Good MUFs will also deftly manage triangular relationships (between them-selves, manager and franchisor) to resolve day-to-day issues.

- **MUF (4–9 units)** – as the number of units grows and they become a 'mini-chain within a chain', the MUF needs to make sure that their organisation has systemised *multi-site* reporting tools that enable them to control/monitor/correct operations. At this stage, the MUF will require part-time professional services support (particularly administration, finance and marketing) although (s)he will have to be careful, keeping central overheads (which are allocated to each unit's P&L) to a minimum due to ongoing expansion costs. From an operational standpoint, MUFs can minimise outlays by appointing a couple of managers as 'cluster' leads, acting as a 'span-breaker' between the MUF and their units.

- **MUF (10+ units)** – now that the enterprise has grown to a suffi-cient scale to support a *modest* central infrastructure, the MUF can hire professional management (operations and training) to sit alongside other head-office services. What successful MUFs do is ensure that their support structure is *integrated* into the broader franchise system (mirroring its roles, functions and duties) to prevent misalignment. Frequently, MUFs have hired support staff from their franchisor as they expand – useful as they are conversant with the service-delivery system and are socialised into the values of the brand. In addition, successful MUFs also ensure that they have proper governance structures in place to underpin what is becoming a sizeable business entity.

But what are the things that really differentiate successful MUFs from under-performing ones? What do the best do to ensure optimal execution of the brand?

- **Right sites** – the most important success factor for MUFs is obvious but requires re-iterating: selecting the right sites for expansion! Often MUFs approach network growth too hastily – being motivated by quantity over quality. At times, it must be said, they are not helped by ambitious franchisors who encourage rapid expansion into unsuitable sites through lucrative one-off incentives. Also, franchisors can sometimes convince MUFs to take on 're-sale' territories that have poorly positioned sites that *cannot* be fixed. Making sub-optimal locational choices will cost the MUF dearly in two respects. First, in acquisition costs and (potentially) running losses; and second, in a diversion of management time that might result in deteriorating performance elsewhere. Successful MUFs wait judiciously for the right sites and opportunities, understanding that a couple of missteps – particularly in the early days of their expansion – could jeopardise their whole livelihood.

- **Incentivise** – one aspect that stands out amongst successful MUFs is the degree to which they 'share their fortune' with their managers/staff through generous compensation/incentive programmes. Incentives and bonuses are tied to key brand KPIs and performance targets but most importantly they are timely, transparent and achievable. Nothing breeds resentment more than managers/staff seeing that they are enriching their MUF through their own efforts for scant reward themselves. Thus, successful MUFs build network resilience and operational excellence by retaining and motivating employees not only through intrinsic means (training, progression, development etc.) but – just as importantly – extrinsic financial mechanisms that guide/ shape desired behaviours.

- **Focus** – as some MUFs grow their network of sites in a 'good' brand, they can lose focus by becoming disrespectful and arrogant (believing that its prosperity is solely down to their brilliance) and/or they 'get bored', using their newly found wealth to diversify into other business interests. The reality – whatever they might think – is that they are contracted members of a formal agreement that has a finite life. If their levels of execution and financial performance (brought about by capital/revenue starvation and a lack of *growth*) tails off they will – at some stage – be brought to account by the franchisor. Successful MUFs do not bite the hand that feeds them; rather, they relentlessly focus on driving and improving their operations!

Case Study 15 – Shadow Structures, Knowledge Transfer and Relationship Management in Select Service Partners (SSP)

Lee Sheldon is the founder of MMU (Mastering Multi-Units), an organisation that trains multi-site operators and advises clients on high-performance multi-unit structures. Previously, Lee was Global Learning and Development Director at SSP (Select Service Partners) which ran managed brands (Millie's and Ritazza) alongside multiple franchised brands (M&S Food, Starbucks, Burger King etc.) at major transport/travel nodes.

In my view, the best MUFs (single and multiple branded franchisees) *design 'tight' shadow structures*, add considerable value by *transferring valuable insights/knowledge* to the franchisor and *create great relationships* through mutual goal attainment. Taking these points in turn…

- **'Tight' shadow structures** – in order to keep down costs, MUFs that run multiple brands (often in single locations) will be tempted to design command structures that provide multiple-branded 'simultaneous cover'. Whilst it is important that service providers on the ground can indeed switch between brands (for efficiency and productivity purposes) the operational teams (at regional director and district level) work most effectively when *they are aligned to specific brands…* enabling them to understand the technical detail, culture and ethos of the brand… interfacing directly with franchisor operational counterparts… Whilst central support (training and marketing) can form part of a 'shared service', as the MUF grows its number of outlets for

CONTINUED …

a specific brand, 'solus' brand concentration becomes vital... Also stability of personnel and job titles are important... I would observe that successful MUFs keep key operational 'linkages' in place for (in this industry!) unusual amounts of time to preserve deep relationships and that – in some cases – mimicking the job titles of the franchisor leads to greater salience and alignment... A single point of senior operational contact between both parties is essential for a successful partnership...

- **Knowledge/information transfer** – often franchisors will have a vast knowledge of how to design and operate so-called 'street-side' brands but might lack knowledge of 'special situations' such as travel nodes... These locations have specific spatial constraints, idiosyncratic trading patterns/'day part' rhythms and differing product/packaging requirements... Multiple-branded MUFs that operate within this space can add great value for franchisor support services, assisting in better designs (queuing, customer order/fulfilment systems), suggesting more efficient staff deployment and rostering (late evening in travel nodes is often equivalent to a lunchtime daypart in 'streetside') and advising on appropriate product ranges and portable packaging (for speed, quality and safety purposes)...

- **Successful relationship** – although it is important that the part-nership is an economic success, this in itself will be an outcome of close 'trust-based' partnership working... This is built up through close collaboration: each side delivering on its prom-ises... listening/respecting the contribution of one another... and in the case of multiple-branded MUFs – agreeing not to poach the franchisor's staff! ... It is quite notable that many MUFs are granted more units over time once they have proved themselves financially; indeed, I have worked for and advised franchisees that have been told that they 'operate the brand better' than the franchisor! ... *why?* ... obviously wishing to retain (and grow) the contract is a large financial incentive for the successful MUF (who will strictly monitor standards and systems adherence) but it is also true to say that MUFs have *less distractions or noise* than the franchisor... they can get on with focussing upon the business of delivering operational excellence day-in, day-out!

CONTINUED ...

> ... Also, from an MUF perspective, relationships are certainly enhanced if the people working in a specific brand are made to feel part of an 'extended family' by the franchisor by being invited to conferences and T&D events, for instance...

THREE KEY 'MUF' FRANCHISEE QUESTIONS

1. Have you selected the right store *growth* opportunities? (The wrong sites will be costly in terms of poor returns and management time.)

2. Do you have proper multi-site infrastructure/incentives in place to achieve operational excellence without direct daily supervision/scrutiny?

3. If you are successful with a large portfolio, have you maintained a sense of perspective, interacting maturely/*respectfully* with your franchisor?

INTERNATIONAL MASTER FRANCHISEE (IMF)

One of the most popular methods format franchises adopt to extend international reach (90% and 70% of US quick service and restaurant franchisors respectively) is through IMF arrangements. These are defined as:

> a form of umbrella licensing agreement which differs from the standard unit or location-level franchise in two ways: (i) it provides for the granting of an exclusive territory extending beyond the trade area of a single unit and (ii) it envisions from the outset the introduction of an additional layer of control between store-level management and the franchisor...
>
> (Kaufmann and Dant 1992: 50)

Franchisors will seek growth outside of their home territories because they are either approaching saturation levels in their domestic market or they have a robust system that works:

> the key capability that predicts the intent to expand overseas is superior capability to reduce franchisee opportunism. Franchisors who

seek foreign franchises have developed a greater capability to bond against and monitor potential franchisee opportunism...

(Shane 1996: 73)

The lowest-risk form of expansion (limited capital outlay allied to control maintenance), the IMF route also enables franchisors to reduce their 'psychic distance' with unfamiliar markets by tapping into the expertise of local 'master' operators – thereby reducing costly 'information gathering costs', cultural misunderstandings and adverse site selection. Obviously, they will have made a pre-assessment of the market ensuring that their target market has a positive economic environment (market size, competitive intensity, demand variability), attractive social environment/culture (franchising acceptance knowledge and entrepreneurial flair) and a robust political/legal system (low corruption and appropriate legal framework).

Typical problems that franchisors encounter when they look at foreign markets (especially in developing/growth terrains) – aside from pure 'macro' market unattractiveness – are insufficient partners of 'suitable calibre' and poor stocks of 'capable' local management. The latter point can be remedied through immersion, modelling and training/development from franchisor personnel but it still remains a perennial problem:

> In a decade examining retail expansion in developing countries, we know that new markets are only as effective as their workforces, and harnessing a local talent pool is crucial to reaching customers. Expatriates deployed from home markets [to help master franchisees] provide much-needed support in the early stages, but long-term success hinges on a skilled, reliable, and affordable local workforce...

(ATKearney 2012: 22)

Inevitably, such issues pose operational/executional problems unless the franchisor chooses the right IMF. But what capabilities do successful IMFs have and which factors are important in determining whether they can successfully *execute* the brand in nuanced/idiosyncratic cultural contexts? The answer to these questions lies in task and partnership-related capabilities:

- **Task-related capabilities**
  - ***Complementary experience*** – often successful IMFs have complementary *product* and *franchising* experience that

makes them extremely valuable partnership material. In terms of the former, they are likely to have operated similar products in their native environment which gives them a familiarity with customer preferences and 'ideal' locations. To the latter point, IMFs who already have a stable of international franchises or have had experience of running one will understand the nature of binding contractual requirements.

- *Managerial/technological capability* – in terms of rolling out the brand, in tandem with the previous point, good IMFs will have (or be able to develop) a management cadre (support and field-based) primed for effective operational execution. In addition, the fact that they might already be operating other franchise systems will mean that they possess sufficient BOH systems/technical capability to perform multi-site compliance and monitoring activities.
- *Financial resources* – in addition to the above, successful IMFs will have sufficient financial resources to service up-front fees and, more importantly, rapid network development.
- **Partnership-related capabilities**
  - *Commitment* – good IMFs will not only 'buy into' the brand but will have a good strategic fit and *compatible goals* with the franchisor. A mutuality of interest will sustain the relationship through inevitable set-backs and mistakes.
  - *Values and trust* – in developing nations, local values/customs/norms might run contrary to 'developed' notions of propriety (examples being self-protective leadership, nepotistic collectivism and covering up to 'save face'). Franchisors must carefully select IMFs with leaders that will share/model their basic values (openness, honesty, integrity and ethical behaviour), given that one of their foremost duties is to protect the brand's reputation. Over time – through honouring their promises and demonstrating strong operational competence – high levels of trust will build between the two parties that will permit the IMF to undertake (further) experimentation with product customisation/adaptation to local conditions (see below).

But what are the winning differentiators for successful IMF execution of the brand?

- **Translation/customisation** – an essential aspect of IMF success is the degree to which, first, the franchisor adapts/translates the *customer-facing elements* of their product to the local market prior to entry and, second, the degree to which the IMF is granted autonomy to make rapid 'in flight' changes that counter *aggressive* imitative/agile local competition and/or changing local preference/tastes. With regard to pre-entry product design, the franchisor would be well-advised (in addition to rigorous local market research) to consult with and listen to their preferred IMF partner. More importantly, following the first pilot stores, it is incumbent on highly *committed* IMFs (who wish to preserve the central integrity of the brand) to make a strong business case to the franchisor for product, service-delivery, marketing and pricing changes that – without diluting the fundamental brand essence – will add demonstrative value.

- **Communication** – one factor that marks out successful relations between the two parties is open dialogue, underpinning close *collaboration*. Distance-related issues (physical, cultural and functional) can give rise to detachment, resentment and misunderstandings – particularly if the venture is underperforming against original expectations. Information asymmetry might occur, with neither side feeling that they are in possession of the 'full facts' and that the other side is 'hiding things'. A solution to this problem that works effectively for several internationalising franchises is 'structural congruence' between franchisor and IMFs: a 'soft' form alignment between 'empowered' support/technical/operational functions from both parties. In addition, the presence of formal communication channels – headed by key decision-makers – will also be in place to resolve issues quickly and amicably (see Chapter 7 below).

Case Study 16 – Master Franchising TGIs and Costa within Eastern Europe

Until 2014, Ian Dunstall was the Senior Vice President Marketing of Rosinter Restaurant Holdings, Russia's largest multi-brand casual dining chain (approximately 360 units – one-third franchised – and 11 brands, including Il Patio, Planet Sushi, Costa Coffee, McDonald's and TGI Friday etc.) operating in 10 countries, spread across 44 cities. Over a successful thirty-year career, Ian previously held several senior executive roles in the restaurant industry.

Given the size of the market, it stands to reason that just about every brand with international aspirations wants to crack Russia and its neighbouring territories… the trouble was that in the early days after the collapse of communism Russia was perceived as something of a 'wild frontier' and brands seeking to enter the market had to look at prospective Russian partners that had the know-how and wherewithal to assist in 'cracking the market'… By the late nineties, Rosinter Restaurants, established by an extremely entrepreneurial local businessman, had established chicken-, pizza- and fish-based concepts – the chicken concept eventually being acquired by KFC – building up a sizeable casual dining company with scale that had seized 'first mover' advantage in Russia… During this time and since, Rosinter has been courted by international brands… eventually developing master franchised and joint venture relationships with TGIs and Costa Coffee, respectively… both these companies had identified Rosinter as an ideal partner – possessing, in their view, the sector experience, geographical knowledge and financial 'firepower' to assist them in building a franchised network within Russia and nearby… However, there are differences in the ways in which the relationships with these two brands have evolved and the relative success they have achieved locally…

In the case of TGIs, a high level of trust enfolded the relationship, through good communications between people and strong mutual goal alignment… its successful relations leading to its Russian interests becoming one of TGIs largest overseas markets (with 36

CONTINUED …

stores)... For although Rosinter had already developed its own 'Americana' offer in its stable (Ambar), it clearly bought into and loved what an authentic, iconic American brand could bring to the market... In the early days it focused upon rolling the brand out in Moscow, then travel hubs (especially airports) and then the regions... It has always had a very strong intent to stay true to the essence of the TGI brand even if – at times – supply chain, language and local management issues have slightly diluted facility and product specifications... The fact that one of the Russian-speaking senior executives at Rosinter had been born in the US certainly aided relations... but I have to say that it was a highly collaborative arrangement... communications were exceptionally good with frequent meetings between key Rosinter staff and TGI's senior EMEA International Franchise team members – in fact, their marketing and communications team provided us with great research and local insight that translated into very effective local campaigns... also many of our people working in the TGIs franchise went to the annual conference in Florida and some gained work experience working in the US... As a consequence, I think our service standards were positive – we recruited for 'zany' personality and implemented the TGI 'earn your stripes' motivational programme (which other businesses across Rosinter certainly learnt a lot from)... Both parties got a lot out of the relationship, I think, and the US parent certainly listened to our concerns when in a corporate identity/logo rebranding it wished to change the iconic red-and-white awnings to black! ...

The Costa relationship was slightly different. The original arrangement was a joint venture partnership that reverted to a straight franchise agreement. Market conditions were different, with well-established Russian brand coffee house competitors who had strong high-street locations with a high proportion of dine-in usage. At the same time, Starbucks was entering the market with a well-funded Kuwaiti multiple franchise operator who had the vision and financial resource for rapid expansion to establish their brand. Whilst Costa would have welcomed similar expansion opportunity, the reality was that the opportunity of Costa for Rosinter was primarily within its transport-hub locations (airport and railway) and as a secondary fill in to existing restaurant locations where there was space available

CONTINUED ...

to squeeze a Costa operation into underutilised space to offset the high rentals. So whilst the Costa operation performed strongly, the expansion vision of the franchisee was probably less than that of the franchisor. Also, in terms of the way the guests used the offer, there was a fundamental difference – a high proportion of users were dine-in rather than coffee-to-go.

So I would say that successful master franchisees do two things well: first, they locate brands that will possess (as in the case of TGIs) clear local differentiation and, second, they are mutually bound to the aspirations and goals of the franchisor... that is to say that they share the same ambition and vision, communicate well... and are financially well-funded to sustain the reputation of the brand (often thousands of miles away!) and execute their 'mutual mission'...

THREE KEY 'IMF' FRANCHISEE QUESTIONS

1. Are you totally *committed* to the roll-out of this brand (buy-in, funding and energy)?
2. Have you got the local capability to make value-added adaptations that do not undermine the core essence of the brand?
3. Are you prepared to *collaborate*/co-operate with the franchisor's international support team?

CHAPTER SUMMARY

This chapter has addressed how different categories of franchisee successfully execute the brand. It has shown how SUFs that adopt a 'hands on' approach can be hampered by scarce resources, whilst MUFs and IMFs – with large contracts at stake – develop an effective infrastructure to 'monitor' and execute the brand. Like the previous chapter, however, there are binding transactional and relational exchange mechanisms that all categories of franchisees deploy to ensure a successful and sustainable partnership with their franchisor during the brand execution process.

In terms of transactional exchange, SUFs (GlassesInc) are more successful when – rather than shirking or free-riding – they relentlessly *comply* with the franchise and brand 'givens' (*product exchange*); MUFs (SSP) are 'given more stores' and permitted to *grow* if they 'prove themselves financially' (*monetary exchange*); and IMFs (Rosinter) foster high levels of '*collaborative* arrangements' by getting their 'key staff' to interact with franchisor 'international franchise team members' (*services exchange*). From a **relational** perspective, SUFs (RetailCo) do better when they are 'open and *honest* about the financials… and *share* local knowledge that might benefit the network' (*information exchange*); MUFs build up 'close "trust-based" partnership working' arrangements with both parties intent upon 'listening/ *respecting* the contribution of one another' (*status exchange*); and IMFs (Rosinter) are aligned with their partner through a 'mutual mission' and are totally *committed* to the cause – 'buy[ing] into and lov[ing]… authentic, iconic' brands (*love exchange*). To some extent this chapter has suggested that during the process of execution, franchisees will have some local autonomy to innovate and contribute to the brand development process. But taking this function as an exclusive area of investigation, how do franchisees – having *engaged* with and *executed* the brand – help *evolve* it as well?

CHAPTER 7
EVOLVE

Following on from *engaging* with and *executing* the brand, the next major activity for franchisees is involvement in the process of *evolving* it. Chapter 4 outlined how franchisors sought to develop the brand in a 'top-down' manner; this section will look at the contribution that franchisees make from a bottom-up perspective. Their active participation in seeking to evolve the brand is unsurprising given their vested economic interest in its success and (in mature systems) the fact that they are – for the most part – a far more permanent fixture than the 'transitory' management that frames the policies:

> franchisees are not single economic actors simply reacting to economic incentive mechanisms but are social actors embedded within a complex set of interpersonal relationships... the formalisation of these relationships into persistent structures such as franchisee associations implies there are additional entities within franchising that are in a position to interpret and frame franchisee incentives and monitoring behaviour for their franchisee members... in mature systems, collective action may well be more likely than individual action when reacting to franchisor initiatives... a maturing US franchise industry has resulted in an environment where an increasing number of franchisees work in franchise systems that are owned by large corporations or private equity groups with high levels of turnover among management. Many of the multi-generational franchisees we encountered in these systems perceive their relationship with the brand as more enduring than those of the current owner or management team...
>
> (Lawrence and Kaufmann 2011: 299)

For sure, given their closer proximity to daily operations, customers and competitors, many franchisees would lay greater claim to 'knowing the business' than 'hired gun' management. But their involvement in evolving the brand lies not just in *influencing central policy* but also in *impacting local strategies* through collaboration with fellow franchisees and through what might be called '*positive opportunism*': seeking new ways and moving the brand forward without the express permission of the franchisor. Of course, their contribution across this range of interventions is pertinent and useful if the franchisee motive is to strengthen the brand rather than service naked self-interest! These three approaches to evolving the brand from a bottom-up perspective will be considered in turn in this chapter.

INFLUENCING CENTRAL POLICY

As stated, most established franchises have formal governance structures that encourage input and participation from franchisees to shape central practices, policies and procedures. The degree to which certain franchisors cynically use these channels as a means of 'pacifying' the network whilst they drive their own agenda is debatable, as is the degree to which successful franchisees can be 'bothered' to get involved! Nonetheless, formal involvement mechanisms with specified articles of association and codes of practice are a feature of strong brands (slightly differing in name/denomination according to history and national domicile). Although the franchisor possesses a high degree of coercive power due to its contractual supremacy, intelligent franchisors understand that (due to distance) they lack expertise regarding certain matters – and therefore exercising referent/relational power (on occasions) through franchisee involvement provides more sustainable outcomes. But what incentives do franchisees have to become involved in these forums? Obviously they have a high 'agency'-based motive to participate in policy-framing activities and intimate operational/market knowledge that can add to the decision-making process. But what kind of participative structures generally exist in franchised brands and how do franchisees successfully contribute to evolving the concept?

- **Consultation** – various mechanisms will exist in most established franchises for franchisees to 'change the system from within'. Usually there are a hierarchy of forums through which franchisees can feed policy/product/opportunity ideas and amendments 'upwards':
  - *Franchise associations* – a franchise association which has elected representatives on regional and local boards that feed into a National Advisory Board is the foremost consultative

mechanism in most franchises. How do franchisees optimise this channel? First, they need to get to know the existing representatives and leadership (president/chairman/officers/secretary/treasurer) to understand franchisee strategy/agenda. Second, they can either give their 'views' to these representatives or opt for election themselves. Generally, franchisees achieve better outcomes when they elect officials that 'match' the situational needs of the brand at any given time (see below).

- *National marketing council* – in addition to franchise associations, the most important consultative forum – given that it is tasked with deploying franchisee marketing fees – is the national marketing council. This committee assists the franchise's marketing function in deciding whether national campaigns should drive awareness through 'halo' campaigns stressing brand attributes or 'penetration' campaigns which stress new products, services and/or special prices (time-bundled promotions). Alongside content, the process of execution and implementation will be discussed with franchisees providing valuable input on operational alignment considerations (i.e. stock and labour to service demand).

- *Standing committees* – in addition to the above, some franchises will also have standing committees where franchisees and/or their representatives (certainly within multiple contexts) can attend meetings chaired by functional heads (i.e. of supply chain, property/estates, operations, training etc.). Such forums give franchisees an opportunity to give 'advice' on certain policies, procedures and initiatives, contributing to the strategy of functional areas. Franchisees usually stand more chance of success in this participative forum when (certainly from an MUF perspective) they match up 'their' experts to those of the franchisor.

- *Other* – further means through which the franchisee can influence franchisor policy include regular surveys (online and telephone), district meetings (see 'Local Agility', below), functions, conferences, online forums and informal interactions (off-the-record meals with franchise leadership, site visits and, personal correspondence etc.). Of all these mechanisms, perhaps one of the most effective means of 'getting the message through' is (surprisingly) face-to-face interaction in 'non-threatening' environments such as meals, where – with 'Chatham House rules' prevailing – powerful members of the network (such as large MUFs) can influence senior policy-makers.

- **Collaboration** – franchisees can also provide significant input to the brand by agreeing to be the test-bed for product, services and policy pilots. Any 'good' franchise has simultaneous trials in place that require the involvement of 'serious' and committed franchisees. Getting involved in this not only affords franchisees an opportunity to shape the future of the brand but also (crucially) to strengthen their relationship with the owner. The effort and resources committed to such endeavours can yield inordinate 'preferential' paybacks!

- **Confrontation** – in extreme circumstances – where the franchise lacks appropriate structures, fails to listen and/or 'loads' committees with highly incentivised 'placemen' – franchisees might have to resort to setting up their own formal structures to influence the franchisor. Sometimes these have taken shape as 'independent franchisee associations' with elected representatives that are mandated to challenge legally opportunistic behaviours from the franchisor (such as unscrupulous price rises in 'must stock' products that directly benefit franchisor revenues/profit). Essentially these structures emerge when there is a notable power asymmetry between the two parties, where the franchisor is perceived to be acting in an inequitable, heavy-handed manner. Do successful franchisees get involved in such structures? The answer lies in whether or not they have proper governance allied to a just cause. Sometimes renegade 'offshoots' are led by charlatans motivated by naked self-interest!

But what are the winning attributes associated with influencing central policy effectively?

- **Situational styles** – it is important that franchisees judge the skills, styles and approaches required by their representatives according to the situation faced by the brand. In benign times, a 'diplomatic' approach may be required: franchisees should look to electing experienced and 'balanced' representatives to advance their cause. During crises a more 'passionate' style will be needed. More aggressive, courageous 'change-making' personalities might be required to fight the 'franchisee corner'.

- **'Sensible' collectivism** – whether franchisees are 'organised' through formal recognised/unrecognised forums, it is important that their elected representatives exercise 'sensible' collectivism. What does this mean? They should seek to represent the 'consensual voice' of the network – eschewing individual agendas – whilst acknowledging that there are inevitably limits to what they can achieve. *Committed* franchisees (who 'love' their brand!) will seek mutually beneficial compromise, which is preferable for beneficial long-term relations, rather than outright victory. Also, concentrating on major issues (that drive revenue/ *growth* or reduce costs) rather than irrelevant minutiae (for petty grandstanding purposes) will strengthen their claims for relevance and influence.

Case Study 17 – Influencing Central Policy in Dunkin' Donuts, Domino's and Snappy Snaps

Andrew Emmerson is the owner of the Emmerson Development Company which advises SMEs and large companies on franchising. Until 2013 he was UK Executive Director of Franchising and Development for Domino's Pizza, having previously held senior executive positions leading/developing/rolling-out Millie's Cookies (UK), Upper Crust (Europe) and Dunkin' Donuts (US). Andrew is currently non-executive chairman of the Snappy Snaps chain, a non-executive at Hotcha and The Victorian Chop House Company, and co-owns three Dunkin' Donuts franchises in the US.

During my long career in franchising I have been on both sides of the table, as franchisor and as franchisee! ... Taking a purely franchisee perspective, what are the best ways of influencing central policy once you are in the system? ... Reflecting upon my past and present involvement with Dunkin' Donuts, Domino's and Snappys, I would highlight three main 'formal' and 'informal' channels of influence for franchisees... although I would argue that 'softer' informal relational means of influence are often more effective than 'hard' transactional formal methods! ...

CONTINUED ...

In my experience, formal channels of influence differ slightly for franchisees according to the culture, history, maturity and scale of the brand... On this basis, Dunkin' Donuts, DPG and Snappy Snaps all had different mechanisms in place for franchisees to influence policy:

- **Consultative** – ... *Dunkin' Donuts* in the US was an extremely mature business with a well-developed set of elected *operational* advisory councils (both regional and national) and elected *marketing* 'ad committees' that were organised according to TV regions (reporting into a national committee) – fulfilling the absolutely crucial role of allocating local/national marketing fees... *Domino's* main consultative forum was the Marketing Advisory Council (MAC) which was populated by elected representatives from specific geographies in addition to the two largest MUFs... At *Snappy Snaps* the Franchisee Leadership Council (FLIC) is a body made up of 12 elected franchisees who advise the franchisor on matters such as operations, marketing spend and franchise agreement amendments...

- **Collaborative** – ... *Dunkin' Donuts* had an excellent system whereby they nominated 'franchisee leaders' – individuals who were influential within their districts and regions – to act as 'go to' people for pilots and tests (such as new operational systems, store designs and product innovation); they did this on the basis that these individuals had a high degree of credibility and so, if they 'gave the nod', the rest of the network would 'buy in'... At Domino's (where we didn't run any stores directly) we regularly used members of the MAC to trial things and be the 'testers' of products... Indeed franchisors who don't run their own stores have few opportunities to try out new programmes in real life... They seek out willing franchisees who will trial new revenue-driving growth (or cost saving!) initiatives that might be of financial benefit to all parties... at the cost of the franchisors, franchisees can have a chance to bring new products or services to their customers and get 'first mover' advantages. Although this (inevitably) leads to operational challenges for the franchisees... with the support of the franchisor (and funds), it is often worth the risk! Plus, again, they can influence the thinking of the brand

CONTINUED ...

owners for the financial benefit of the entire system. The same is true with the members of *Snappy Snaps* FLIC, although we have the additional advantage of having three owned stores at present in which we can new test product and design... Over the years, I have worked with several franchisees whose willingness to try things brought them and the brand significant benefits! ...

- **Confrontational** – ... in highly mature brands – where growth is driven through organic incrementalism rather than store roll-out programmes – high levels of tension can exist between both parties because franchisees (prevented by saturation from taking on extra territories) become frustrated over 'misfiring' central growth initiatives... When franchisees believe that the organisation has stopped listening to them or has 'loaded' advisory committees with 'patsies', they can do two things: either deselect their nominated representatives and replace them with more assertive characters who are more in tune with 'franchisee sentiment'... or (in extremely rare cases) set up independent associations that take independent advice on how to counter unpopular franchisor initiatives ('class actions' being the last resort)...

These (differing) formal methods of influencing central policies, practices and procedures are highly useful for franchisees... but I strongly maintain – having been on both sides of the fence – that one of the best ways of 'shaping' franchisor policies is informally, outside of normal structures! ... For instance:

- **Profitable deviance** – ... I have known franchisees that have 'loved' their brand and experimented... committed to make things better ... without asking permission but seeking forgiveness afterwards! ... One case that springs to mind is an extremely experienced franchisee who – concerned with COG inflation – 'unbundled' a core offer saving 6% in 'dish costs' with no impact on sales! ... He then presented this back to the organisation who adopted this as standard... Obviously, the marketing people weren't happy at first... but the point was that this MUF bravely experimented with the best of intentions, proved it worked and then 'sold' it into the centre and the rest of the organisation...

CONTINUED ...

- **Courageous expertise** – ... again, I have known experienced franchisees who have bypassed formal channels of influence and – using their deep knowledge and expertise – have altered policy by courageous 'direct interaction' with senior franchisor personnel... One case springs to mind... A franchisor had proposed changes to the Franchise Agreement that were more 'lawyer' than 'operator' friendly! ... By taking direct action – camping outside the CEO's office – the franchisee was able to get an 'audience' and present hard empirical evidence relating to 'unintended consequences' that could be harmful for both parties... ultimately achieving major revisions!

- **'Humanising' relations** – ... 'Grown up' franchisees can also affect policy through forming deep bonds with franchisor personnel... the more intimate human relations become within a business context – the more fruitful the outcomes for both parties... getting to know one another well – understanding hopes/desires/fears – leads to greater trust and mutual respect... 'Serious' franchisees have invited me to social events (family functions such as weddings and parties) which increased our mutual understanding... Also, I often found that good franchisees who attended company functions/ceremonies and talked to me over a drink or two in the bar... could (in this unthreatening/open environment) get their points over as to how the company could be more successful... I learnt a lot from these conversations – often more so than from sitting on committees and councils! ...

THREE KEY 'CENTRAL INFLUENCING' FRANCHISEE QUESTIONS

1. Do you feel that you are *committed* and can contribute to the future *growth* and prosperity of the brand? (Have you got the right mindset?)

2. Are you actively involved in the democratic structures of the brand and/or do you have close personal relations with key decision makers? (Both are important.)

3. Have you signed up to trial and test new initiatives that will either *grow* sales or reduce costs?

LOCAL AGILITY

Seeking to evolve the brand at a strategic level is important but successful franchisees also attend to enhancing the brand's status, recognition and reach at a local level. Achieving a degree of local agility and responsiveness is critical. In order to do so, however, they must act in concert with both the franchisor and, in all likelihood, other franchisees. Obvious problems for franchisees in attempting some kind of local flexibility, relate to the degree of brand rigidity/uniformity and the latitude afforded for some element of customisation. Previous sections (see 'International Master Franchisee' in Chapter 6) have referred to instances when the franchisor has to grant permission for adaptation to customer-facing products/services for cultural reasons. But what about standard franchises operating in home markets? As stated previously, no store faces *exactly* the same contextual and environmental issues (demographics, position, layout, competition etc.). In addition, franchisees are constantly faced with the dilemma of how to reinvent and 'freshen' themselves – creating compelling reasons to visit from both existing and (more crucially) new customers. Adopting centrally conceived tools and initiatives will go some way to addressing some of these needs but, often, successful franchisees will be extremely adept at utilising formal and informal local processes to attack proximal markets. What are these channels and how do 'winning' franchisees successfully leverage them?

- **Formal channels** –
  - ***Area franchisee meetings*** – gaining ideas for increasing local impact and awareness can be derived from 'area meetings' at which the FSM will lead an agenda that – having primarily addressed central initiatives – will then move onto an 'open forum' where franchisees can share best practice ideas. Chapter 4 described how knowledge transfer between parties could be encouraged by the FSM, but it is essentially up to franchisees to exchange/reciprocate insights/information in order to obtain some added value. Hoarders of information are deluding themselves if they believe that 'not sharing' is the best way to advance their businesses.
  - ***Marketing co-operative*** – a district marketing association (DMA) is an important forum for franchisees to pool their resources at a local level in order to fill 'slack' times in the annual marketing calendar, support national campaigns and/ or address local competitive threats. These committees

(governed by strict by-laws) are successful when they design local campaigns/initiatives that emphasise points of difference with competitors, 'spoil' competitor campaigns and are properly costed/implemented/assessed for promotional impact.

- *Business plans* – at an individual store level, franchisees will also work with their FSMs on tailored activity to animate/improve sales. Whilst this will include some element of marketing, it will inevitably address some of the operational 'hygiene factors' relating to the business (see Chapter 4). Inevitably, successful franchisees draw upon all available resources from both central and field-based resources to enhance their offer. They are also proactive in raising the local profile and reputations of their business through active community engagement: charity work, PR and tie-ups with other retailers. The degree to which they also integrate local and national plans – ensuring symmetry/alignment – is another major determinant of success.

- **Informal channels** –
  - *Franchisee exchange* – a useful way of seeking ideas to evolve and improve the local offer is through local network sharing and 'peer-to-peer cross-learning' (through meetings, site visits, e-mails, phone calls etc.). If franchisees can overcome their natural competitive tendencies (exacerbated by league tables and in-company competitions/challenges) and 'not invented here' egos, there is a high value to be gained from exchanging information amongst themselves and 'training their fire' at the competition rather than against one another. For SUFs, it also eases isolation and the burden of working alone whilst MUFs gain some useful hints and tips as to how they can run more effectively a 'chain within a chain'. If franchisees agree – before they 'share' soft (information and people) and hard (machinery and technology) resources – that they will not poach one another's key staff, such exchanges are grounded upon even firmer foundations.

But what are the key differentiators for evolving the local offer through agile behaviours?

- **Personal characteristics** – in the section 'Franchised Mindset' in Chapter 5, reference was made to the need for successful franchisees to possess certain key attributes including agreeableness, conscientiousness (to *comply* with the brand 'givens'), emotional stability and entrepreneurism. The latter trait is absolutely critical in determining local agility which – in itself – requires *curiosity* (to scan), courage (to try) and persistence (to carry on) on the part of the franchisee. Those that sit back and expect the central brand team to deliver all they require in terms of profit and revenue growth are misguided. Local passivity is a recipe for decline and failure. Proactive attempts to improve relentlessly all aspects of the offer in order to optimise the local market are a critical ingredient of franchisee success. Those that adopt the latter approach invariably possess the aforementioned personal characteristics.

- **Harnessing staff** – whilst ideas can be can be derived from central/field-based support staff and other franchisees, another important source of knowledge resides within the franchisee's direct team. Frontline service providers, BOH production (in food service), shift/section managers and general managers (in the case of MUFs) provide an invaluable source of intelligence and insight. For instance, Di Pietro and colleagues' comparison between MUFs and their general managers found due to service proximity:

> in service quality, franchisees appeared to have less empathy than managers... A franchisee has to deal with many more factors external to the actual daily operations of a business and therefore is likely in many less situations requiring the activation of empathy whereby managers must deal with a great deal of situations that empathy are important to (e.g. service recovery, employee lack of performance, employee not on time etc. ...)

(Di Pietro et al. 2008: 76)

Franchisees that encourage listening and insight *sharing* – harnessing the views, opinions and ideas of their people who have a greater understanding of customer needs due to direct daily interaction – are more likely to be locally agile than their peers.

Case Study 18 – Evolution and Exchange in Café2U

Alex Dawson was firstly a consultant (2005–7) and then Operations Director (2007–11) for Café2U, a master-franchised artisan coffee and food-to-go mobile concept which grew from start-up to 55 vans operated by 48 franchisees in 40 UK and Irish urban conurbations. An experienced leisure operator, Alex has held multi-site management and brand development roles in some of the UK's fastest-growing hospitality organisations and is a graduate of the BCU Multi-Unit Leadership Programme.

The Café2U story is a fascinating one which encompasses two growing trends in the UK: mobile concessions and artisan coffee... The founder of the brand in the UK was at university with me and spotted the Café2U business when he was in Australia... Coming back to the UK he signed a master-franchise agreement with the company to establish the concept in the UK, buying and setting up his own van to experiment and hone the brand – making it fit for purpose in the UK. I came onboard as a consultant helping him refine and roll out the concept about six months later... Really there are two parts to the story... first, there is the *evolution* of the franchise – the way in which the product and brand evolved over time whilst I was there... second, the degree to which the *exchange* of information and knowledge improved over time between 'the centre' and the franchisees, and amongst the franchisees themselves...

- **Evolution** – the core insight of the brand... its differentiated positioning... was providing the '*theatre of freshly made full-bean coffee*' from a mobile platform accompanied by quality hot/cold food-to-go... Our target markets in the initial phases were business parks with white-collar workers, although as appreciation/education for full-bean coffee grew during the mid-noughties we also tapped into industrial estate and factory locations... at one point we were tempted into trying fixed-station pods, but the associated overheads and immobility proved major issues and we got back to core! ... Gradually, as we sold franchised territories (franchisees having to invest in the equipment, pay a modest fixed weekly licence fee and a small marketing fee, and being

CONTINUED ...

tied into buying certain 'must stock' products), our franchisees opened up and spotted new markets – most notably the fast-growing events market in the UK... However, it is fair to say that both the brand and aspects of the product evolved over time:

- *Brand* – at first – during the experimentation stage – our franchisor took a benevolent approach to our branding... which at the time was fairly 'loose'... over time, as we grew, we tightened up our official liveries (on the vans, menus, packaging and marketing) and adhered to the product standards and obligations outlined in the Franchise Agreement and Operations Manual... This presented a far more professional image to our franchisor, customers and prospective franchisees (where interest grew as we entered the credit crunch in 2008 and people were seeking alternative employment options)... It also gave our franchisor greater faith in our ability to execute the 'basics' well – granting us extra latitude to experiment with the offer...

- *Offer* – over time, although the coffee offer remained constant (with the exception of different 'flavour' additions), we experimented constantly with the food offer... We had to take account of demographics, occasion and local tastes... For instance, what worked in cosmopolitan urban areas (local, fresh and healthy) didn't sell elsewhere and different dayparts/occasions (especially outdoor events) also required the right 'food-to-go' fit...

- **Exchange** – as we grew, we needed to communicate more effectively with our franchisor and franchisees in order to keep both parties onboard... Interaction with our franchisor became more frequent as we became more successful – sharing vital information with them to retain good relations was essential... For our franchisees, giving them a say in matters so that they felt that they had some power within the system and were benefitting from best-practice sharing... also getting the franchisees to exchange information themselves:

  - *Central mechanisms* – in terms of direct communications, as the network grew we had a regular newsletter (News2U), intranet, workshops, national meetings, and eventually an

CONTINUED ...

annual national conference... We also adopted the Australian model of a franchise advisory council (FAC) which was comprised of a chairman and two franchisee representatives (all elected)... management's only involvement was as minute takers... the main duties of the FAC were to allocate the central marketing fund and pick up any issues that their franchise members had... This forum was extremely important, giving franchisees the sense that they had a 'voice' and some sort of mechanism to influence policy and strategy...

- *Local Mechanisms* – as the network grew and franchisees (predominantly owner–managers with a few small multiples) met one another at events and training sessions, so their informal links with one another grew... Two mechanisms were really useful in getting franchisees to share ideas: regional meetings and the intranet messaging board... we held four regional meetings back-to-back around the UK where we got clusters of franchisees together to share their ideas with both us and one another – a two-hour meeting was always followed by a meal where people could relax and 'bond'... the intranet messaging board was a really useful vehicle for franchisees with questions, problems or issues (say with local marketing issues and event organisation) to gain insightful responses from others that had already 'been there, done that, got the tee-shirt!'... Also I know that as relationships formed between franchisees, ideas and knowledge flowed on an informal, ad hoc basis between parties as trust-based relationships built up over time...

Franchising in the UK is not as established as it is in Australia or the US (partly due to funding, reputational and image issues), so being a master franchisee – getting the franchise off the ground in the UK in the early days – was a real challenge... The business survived and really prospered during the recession (when several new ambitious and entrepreneurial franchisees came on board) and – as I am still closely connected to some franchisees in the brand – I am delighted to say that it is still evolving and doing well today! ...

THREE KEY 'LOCAL AGILITY' FRANCHISEE QUESTIONS

1. Are you *complying* with the base 'hygiene' factors of the brand which will grant you licence for more local autonomy?

2. Are you reciprocating/*sharing* ideas with your local peers to increase your sales or reduce your costs?

3. Are you utilising the 'talents of all your team' to harness ideas for better 'ways of working', driving sales and connecting with your customers?

POSITIVE OPPORTUNISM

The franchising literature views opportunism as a negative franchisee behaviour – largely being connected with value-destructive instances of 'shirking' and 'free-riding'. There are extreme occasions, however, when opportunistic behaviours can be interpreted in a more positive way. Reference has previously been made to the fact that, given the distance of the franchisor from its units, its failure – at times – to use (or listen to) franchisee expertise in the conception of new change initiatives, coupled with its lack of insight into the minutiae of unit operations (due to few operators transitioning into jobs 'in the centre'), some franchisor change initiatives might be ill-conceived or badly thought out. The franchisee now has a choice: does (s)he accept the change initiative lock, stock and barrel or seek to make (legal) alterations that make the initiatives more workable? For sure many franchisees, fearing sanctions from the franchisor for non-compliance, will adopt the former route, passively accepting what they 'have been told to do'. Braver, more self-confident franchisees (a state usually borne through scale, track record and experience) will, however, not accept the status quo, making adaptations themselves following consultation with their team ('patch-ups'), ignore initiatives completely deploying more effective solutions ('workarounds') or autonomously employ radical solutions to problems that fall outside permitted rules and procedures (added value deviance). These forms three forms of positive opportunism will be considered in turn.

- **'Patch ups'** – in the first instance, successful franchisees will make modifications by 'patching up' the deficiencies of a change initiative. This means that having understood the detail of the proposal and consulted with their team, (s)he will sanction improvements that will add value to both the *content* and *process* of the change initiative. With regard to *content*, franchisees might make alterations that make the initiative more impactful. In terms of *process*, franchisees might speed up or slow down the time-table of certain initiatives and the manner in which they are rolled out. In doing so, they will have taken into account factors such as capacity or 'bandwidth' and the relative priority of certain initiatives in relation to others promulgated by the franchisor. At times, the franchisee might not be acting unilaterally but will be acting in sync with what already might have been agreed at area level after discussion with the FSM and their peers.

- **'Workarounds'** – in exceptional circumstances, franchisees effectively will 'work around' certain initiatives because of their perceived value-destructive nature. This is not to say that they fully reject the concepts and aims underpinning the initiative. 'Workarounds' fulfil the main intentions or *ends* of the initiative without any resort to the *means* suggested by the policy designers. This is a highly dangerous strategy that, in the hands of inexperienced or over-excited franchisees, can foster and embed bad behaviour. Living solely by the dictum that 'the ends justify the means' can lead to chaos and anarchy in stand-ardised franchised contexts. Nonetheless, there are instances where, after mature and rational consideration, implementing a 'work around' strategy can pay dividends. Usually, successful franchisees will gain permission from higher authorities before embarking on such a course of action in order to eliminate penalty or punishment.

- **Added-value deviance (AVD)** – on a very few occasions, successful (maverick!) franchisees will breach company stand-ards, rules and procedures if they believe that either the 'law is an ass' or that there are better ways of doing things. This behav-iour can be termed 'added-value deviance' because, whilst such behaviour might be deemed illegal by the organisation, it might actually serve to improve the performance of operations. As stated, some franchisees might be well ahead of techno-crats at the centre in terms of what the customer expects and what might give them competitive advantage within local micro-markets. Indeed, sometimes the franchisor's field operatives will conspire to give tacit approval to breaches that add manifest value. It is important to state however that added-value deviance will only flourish under two conditions. First, it is only operable or sustainable within 'circles of trust' where franchisees feel that they are protected by higher authorities who will shield them against punishment. Second, a strict code of personal conduct must apply. Short-termist, self-interested 'blatant cheating' will have harmful long-term side effects on the network. There are some instances when over-exuberant (or desperate) franchisees have instituted policies in their own interests that 'have blown up the machine'.

But what are the differentiators that sets apart 'positive' from 'negative' opportunism?

- **Value added** – the narrative above states that all positive opportunism needs to be value added but this requires reiterating and reinforcing. Value added for whom? Negative opportunism is counterproductive for the whole system as franchisees capitalise upon the efforts of others rather than of themselves. Positive opportunism is where franchisees genuinely try to improve matters or do things better/more effectively, sharing their results/insights in a collaborative manner with others. To this extent, their actions – although rule-breaking – are enshrouded within a code of morality and ethics where the best outcomes are sought to strengthen, not weaken, the brand.

- **Trust** – as stated, on many occasions the franchisee will act opportunistically with the *tacit* approval of higher authorities that share their frustrations concerning centre-unit inertia, detachment and breakdown. It is vitally important that franchisees do not abuse this trust by *disrespecting* others and taking advantage of their privileged position, boasting and/or 'going beyond the pale'. Franchisees that do so will quickly find that the rules and sanctions that enfold their contractual arrangements will be applied against them forcibly with wide support from their peers.

Case Study 19 – Deviating from the Brand Standard: Filling Dayparts at Ramada Encore

Until 2014, Kelly Grimes was the Operations Director of the multiple franchisee organisation New World Hotels (NWH), responsible for opening and running four 'premium value' Ramada Encore Hotels in the UK. In a twenty-five-year career in hotels, Kelly had previously worked for Holiday Inn and Hilton.

In the early noughties, Wyndham, the owner of the Ramada hotel chain, decided – having analysed the success of Holiday Inn Express and Premier Inn in the UK – to devise and roll out a chain of budget hotels. They adopted a franchised model for roll out, signing up two franchised multiples to deliver a total of approximately 26 units... The design specification for the brand was tight: set colour schemes (blue, red, yellow and green), defined standards for bedrooms, bathrooms, reception and bar... its differentiating aspects (from its competitive set) being wet-room bathrooms, wooden-floored bedrooms and wardrobes without doors – so-called 'minimalist chic'! ... Once the first hotels were built and operating to these pre-set design specifications, the Ramada central team checked on operational standards and systems execution (i.e. reservation system usage, rate parities, loyalty club displays, complaint resolution etc.) through annual 'hotel engagement' and spontaneous quality audits (mystery-customer based)...

We opened our first hotel in Crewe in 2008 right at the start of the credit crunch, with another three following soon afterwards... Obviously, trading for all hotel operators was challenging and we needed to seek ways of generating incremental revenue... not least to service our debts and recoup our investment at NWH... One of the ways we did this was to *deviate* from the 'softer' brand standards (service delivery and ancillary products)... The question I always posed to the GMs, rather than 'what are the brand requirements?', was 'what does the customer really value/want – what additional services can we provide to satisfy needs?'... After all, our sites were all different (airport, motorway junctions etc.) having idiosyncratic local features/needs... Three examples spring to mind where we

CONTINUED ...

deviated from brand standards in order to *sweat the assets* and their *business 'dayparts'* effectively…

- **Room service** – Ramada Encore had a 'lean' service standard: for instance, customers had to collect the ironing board from reception, collect their own food and/or dine in the bar restaurant… Given that many of our customers were 'singletons', business people who felt uncomfortable eating in public spaces alone, offering a simple room-service offer (serviced by the staff we already had on-site) – although outside specification – added real value… giving us approximately £10k per month over the four sites! …

- **Events** – again, offering meeting conference rooms for events (weddings, christenings, evening receptions, birthdays, Xmas parties etc.) was not part of the initial brand standard… However, for people that were looking to do events 'on a budget' – our sites were perfect… Taking pictures of the rooms when they were properly 'dressed' and locally marketing our facilities was particularly successful in sites like Barnsley where Ramada Encore was perceived as being far more upmarket than some of the other options… It also built links with the community and established the hotels as well-known local amenities… One site catered for 25 events that – with an average revenue of £1.5K – generated approximately £75k! …

- **Free Wi-Fi** – at the start, free Wi-Fi was not part of the brand standard but we had trading dayparts we needed to fill between breakfast and lunch (10.00–12.30) and lunch and dinner (14:00–18:00). Installing Wi-Fi so that business people could use the hotels between meetings or destinations encouraged traffic at 'dead times'… This business generated extra F&B revenue… It was such a successful initiative that Ramada adopted it as a brand standard shortly afterwards…

Why were we able to deviate from original brand standards? … First, we never did anything to harm the reputation of the wider Ramada brand – on the contrary, we co-opted more customers for Encore! … Second, our revenue-driving initiatives generated more royalty fees for Ramada and some great ideas (such as free Wi-Fi)

CONTINUED …

for their central/field support functions... Third, we stuck rigidly to the core 'hygiene' standards of the brand (fixtures and fittings, merchandising, reservations etc.)... Fourth, because of strong competitive pressures from far larger chains and Ramada Encore's 'thin' consumer franchise (due to a small UK footprint), we were given (tacit) licence to deviate from the standard... Fifth, given that my actual employers are NWH, it was incumbent on me to drive the businesses so that we were perceived as a successful MUF... worthy of more sites and investment! ...

THREE KEY 'POSITIVE OPPORTUNISM' QUESTIONS

1. Do your actions serve to strengthen or harm the brand? (Either through 'gorging' or cheating stakeholders)

2. When you discover value-added 'patch-ups', 'workarounds' and initiatives, do you *collaborate* with the franchisor and your peers, sharing your learning?

3. Although 'you do not ask permission but seek forgiveness!' have you got sufficient 'air cover' from strong 'internal allies' (should things go awry)?

CHAPTER SUMMARY

This chapter has outlined how franchisees can assist the franchisor in evolving their businesses and brand to achieve mutual benefit from both top-down (implementing central policy) and bottom-up (local agility and positive opportunism) perspectives. In themselves, the latter sections are an important contribution because most previous books on franchising assume that change is centrally co-ordinated rather than 'seeping up' from store level. However, we should not be surprised by this. Chapter 5 (Engage) described how – in the words of the Spar respondent – franchisors sought to recruit franchisees with a 'schizophrenic' combination of 'conformist' and 'creative' behaviours! Franchisors should therefore be unsurprised when some of their franchisees attempt to 'push the envelope' by evolving matters at a local level. But what do the texts and case studies above tell us about how franchisees bolster their attachment/partnership with their franchisor? Again, analysis of the main themes suggests that franchisees resort to both **transactional** and **relational exchange** mechanisms to strengthen ties between the two parties.

From a **transactional** perspective, franchisees wishing to 'influence central policy' (Snappy Snaps/Dunkin' Donuts) transacted with their owners by willingly trialling centrally conceived 'revenue-driving' *growth* (or cost saving!) initiatives that could 'influence the thinking of the brand owners for the financial benefit of the entire system' (*monetary exchange*); achieved a high degree of 'local agility' (Café2U) in return for *complying* to hygiene factors – 'adhering to product standards and obligations outlined in the Franchise Agreement and Operations Manual' (*product compliance exchange*); and *collaborated* with 'central/field support functions' by passing on 'revenue-driving' ideas flowing from 'positive opportunism' (Ramada Encore) (*services exchange*).

Likewise, from a **relational** standpoint, franchisees attempting to 'influence central policy' (Snappy Snaps/Dunkin' Donuts) showed that they 'loved' their brand by 'experimenting', '*committed* to make things better!' (*love exchange*); during the exercise of 'local agility', franchisee interactions with the franchisor became more (rather than less) frequent so that 'vital information' could be *shared* to 'retain good relations' (*information exchange*); and 'positive opportunism' (Ramada Encore) was exercised with *respect*, on the express understanding that 'deviation' shouldn't involve anything that could 'harm the reputation of the wider... brand and system' (*status exchange*).

CHAPTER 8
CONCLUSION

This book has been a modest attempt to explore how both parties (the franchisor and franchisee) *mutually* succeed in retail franchising. As the Introduction stated, franchising is becoming a more popular route for business expansion for new and existing retail formats in the UK and internationally, reducing brand owners' capital outlay/risk and offering 'entry-bound' small-business start-ups greater certainty of financial success through a proven business model. To date, however, there has been a limited amount of *broad empirical* enquiry into why retail franchise concepts succeed or fail. *Practitioner* books are largely 'how to' guides written by people who base their insights upon acquired personal experience or extensive activity (consulting, teaching and advising) in the franchised domain. From an *academic* perspective, research has tended to have a *narrow* focus – concentrating on discreet aspects of franchised critical success factors. Exceptions exist of course (the seminal book by Spinelli et al. 2004 being a notable example) but the authors embarked on this book with the view – endorsed by many in the franchising industry – that there was a gap in the market for a book based on extensive contemporaneous case-study research that could add to the sum of knowledge in this area.

But what does this book say and how does it advance our understanding of retail franchising success? This chapter will, first, reprise the structure and overarching themes that resonate throughout the book. Second – building upon the insights from each chapter summary – this concluding chapter will advance and expand upon a new model of *franchised social exchange* which the authors believe serves as a (universal) explanation of the dominant question of this book, namely: how can 'both parties win' in retail franchising?

BOOK STRUCTURE AND THEME

This book started with a review of the academic literature which offers up *transactional*, *relational* and *developmental* explanations for franchised success/failure. *Transactional* explanations were shown as being mainly located in economic and legal perspectives, with success being contingent upon strong incentives and contract equity which reduce search/monitoring costs, moral hazard, free-riding, shirking and levels of opportunism. *Relational* perspectives in the academic literature assumed psychological and sociological perspectives. From a psychological standpoint, franchising success is deemed to be connected to the psychological climate between partners, levels of attachment between parties, the expecations of nascent franchisees, perceived levels of support, degrees of job satisfaction, communication/goal alignment and appropriate franchisee profiling/personalities. The sociological dimension stresses the importance of balanced power resouces between parties (particularly through joint-decision-making stuctures) to minimise perceptions of coercion and the engenderment of reciprocity/exchange between partners to reduce conflict. *Developmental* explanations rooted in strategic, marketing and international perspectives stress the importance of executive (rather than partcipative) leadership, the importance of promoting a learning culture, channelled methods of brand distribution (particularly through MUFs), effective organisational configuration with strong support expertis, and customised approaches in international contexts as key determinants of success.

Reviewing this literature, it was concluded that, as useful as these academic explanations and perspectives were, two major gaps were apparent: *first*, an absence of an integrated framework that brought all these strands together (many of the concepts and insights being inter-related rather than mutually exclusive!) and, *second*, a lack of contemporaneous case studies that give a voice to *both* parties in the relationship (most studies having examined franchisor rather than franchisee success factors).

In order to address these gaps, this book then posited an overarching structure for the succeeding narrative (see Figure 8.1 below). This structure was based around the dominant *activities* of both parties which – in themselves – captured *critical success factors* within the retail franchising domain. The book then proceeded to unpack these activities and critical success factors which were shaped/moulded by the mediating social exchange mechanisms between the two parties. Indeed, as Figure 8.1

shows in pictorial form, franchisor and franchisee activities and critical success factors are not only 'matched' side-by-side but have mutual dependencies through SET (social exchange theory) forces (diagrammatically highlighted through the arching arrows).

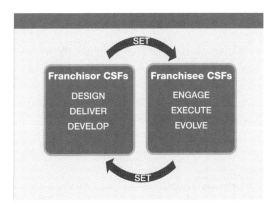

Figure 8.1: Franchising Critical Success Factor Framework

As the book progressed, outlining the hygiene/differentiating success factors for each activity, backed up by illuminating case studies from a variety of businesses/respondents (which posed a number of key questions for franchisors and franchisees reading this book), a key theme emerged which validated the importance of social exchange theory as a principal force in determining good/bad outcomes. This theme (echoing the observations of previous commentators) was one of trust-based *interdependence*: the feeling by case-study respondents that success in retail franchising rested in acknowledging, addressing and leveraging 'trust-centred' *mutuality* between the two parties:

> I have always believed that you can only build a successful and sustainable franchised business by adopting a *'win–win'* mentality which builds trusting, long-term relationships…

> Chris Moore, ex-CEO Domino's (Case Study 1)

This sentiment was echoed in nearly every subsequent case study with respondents referring to the importance of fostering/encouraging trust-based 'joint interest', 'mutual goals', 'mutual self-interest', 'mutually bound aspirations', 'symbiosis', 'partnership' and 'togetherness' between parties as a basis for commercial success. But how is such a state of heightened trusting mutuality and interdepedence achieved, improved and sustained?

SOCIAL EXCHANGE – HOW BOTH SIDES CAN WIN

Hopefully, to many readers, this book will provide a useful reference guide to the 'dos and don'ts' of retail franchising. In many of the sections, pithy checklists are provided with supporting case-study materials and questions. It is our task as researchers, however, to build upon or extend our frontiers of knowledge in retail franchising – and the case-study material in this book provides us with an excellent means of doing so. The question at the end of the last section asked how trust-based interdependencies between the two parties could be optimised. The answer to this reverborated throughout the case-study accounts – locating/validating (see Figure 8.1) *social exchange as the major 'binding' mechanism* between the two parties. But – as a reminder – what is social exchange theory in franchising?

> **Social exchange theory** is premised on acceptance of social norms in interpersonal interactions and is typically defined by the expectations that exchange members have regarding behaviour. These exchanges between partners are driven by self-interest, characterised by **co-operation and reciprocity**, and lead to **mutually beneficial economic and/or non-economic outcomes**. This is relevant to franchising, whereby franchisor and franchisee interaction centres on episodic exchanges entrenched in a **mutually beneficial relationship** such that both parties adapt to one another for equitable outcomes. Social exchange theory is related to Homan's (1961) exchange theory, which suggests individuals will **reciprocate positively or negatively, to what they receive** in a business relationship…
>
> (Harmon and Griffiths 2008: 257)

This notion of trusting/successful mutuality being guided and influenced by positive or negative reciprocity in exchange relations is continually reinforced by the case-study accounts in this book. Indeed, what emerges (after exhaustive analysis and cross-correlation of texts) is what can be termed as a franchise exchange model (FEM) which helps to explain how both sides can win in retail franchising. The sections below will, first, outline the putative model and, second, explain its constituent parts using case-study material.

FRANCHISE EXCHANGE MODEL

The main contribution of this book is not that it overturns or dismisses observations made by previous commentators and academics about the main tenets of successful franchisor–franchisee relations. Rather, it builds a more integrated model which explains how both sides can win. The literature review in the Introduction highlighted how important 'transactional' (tangible economic) and 'relational' (non-tangible behavioural) forces were in the franchised inter-party dynamic. This was endorsed in an insightful opening case study in which Chris Moore, an ex-CEO of Domino's, referred to the importance of franchisors paying due regard to behavioural EQ (emotional intelligence) and 'number grinding' economic IQ to achieve a 'win–win' situation with their franchisees. But what types of 'transactional' and 'relational' currencies are exchanged by both parties?

As discussed in the Introduction, social scientists have established that business relations are predominantly goverened by six main *archetypes of exchange*, namely: *money, product/goods* and *services* (which can be defined as transactional currencies of exchange) and *love, information* and *status* (relational exchange types). The summaries of each chapter pinpointed examples where these forms of archetypal exchange were traded by each party. Furthermore, there seemed to be converging features of exchange within these archetypes that related *specifically* to successful franchisor–franchisee interaction. Figure 8.2, below, highlights the main business exchange archetypes previously highlighted by eminent scholars, with specific franchisor–franchisee 'trade-off' exchange mechanisms which have emerged from this research located with each archetype.

Business Exchange Archetypes		Franchise Exchange Mechanisms	
		Franchisor	Franchisee
Transactional	Money	Incentives	Capital & Growth
	Product/Goods	Quality	Compliance
	Services	Expertise	Collaboration
Relational	Love	Recognition	Commitment
	Status	Inclusivity	Respect
	Information	Honesty	Sharing

Figure 8.2 – Franchise Exchange Model

What Figure 8.2 outlines – drawing on the empirical evidence of the case studies in this book – is how trust-based interdependence is forged between retail franchise partners through a number of reciprocal mechanisms. Further explanation as to *what* they are, *why* they are important and *how* they have been surfaced (through case-study analysis) is provided below.

TRANSACTIONAL MECHANISMS

Transactional archetypes of exchange between business partners encompass 'hard' tangible economic items such as *money, product/goods* and *services*. In retail franchising these archetypes can be recast as franchise exchange mechanisms, eliciting positive/negative reciprocation between partners (see Figure 8.2). To a certain extent they can be viewed as extrinsic, hygiene factors for the relationship – imbalances leading to a lack of trust, disengagement, resistance and/or sabotage.

I. MONETARY EXCHANGE

The first exchange archetype in business relations is money – the base foundation for commercial relations. As businesses are financially based entities built around a profit motive, monetary exchanges must be fair and balanced for the sake of harmony and sustainability. In the case of retail franchising, as the case studies (and indeed the literature) demonstrate, franchisors must exchange sufficient monetary *incentives* with franchisees for optimal outcomes – whilst franchisees must reciprocate by deploying appropriate *capital* whilst seeking to *grow* revenues (ergo franchisor fees).

- **Incentives (Franchisor)**

  Types of franchisor 'incentive mechanisms' highlighted in the case studies included: business model profitability (to attract and retain), equitable share of the 'profit pool' (to engage and motivate), extra store opportunities for high performers (to reward/ replicate excellence) and one-off 'animating' incentives (that shape desired behaviours). Proof that these forms of franchisor incentives are critical resonated throughout the franchisor case studies, primary examples including:

The financial model is extremely stable: energy consumption and staff costs are reduced and the division of labour allows for the raising of productivity…

Misha Zelman, Burger & Lobster (Case Study 2)

[T]he way in which you 'divide up the profit pig' is also critical… to my mind a proper share that worked for DPG (as a quoted company) was 1/3 (franchisor), 2/3 (franchisee)… we also rewarded the best by offering them store growth opportunities…

Chris Moore, Domino's (Case Study 1)

Musgrave had an astonishingly frank and benevolent core value of 'don't be greedy'… they believed in long-term sustainable relationships with their franchisees based on mutual respect founded upon a fair 'division of the spoils'… [they] were quite keen to lock their franchisees in with 'chains of gold' [ensuring] they didn't move to other symbol franchised groups and operated the franchise to unbelievably high standards (a must, given the 'fresh quality' ethos of the brand)…

Paul Daynes, Musgrave (Case Study 5)

Every six months we analyse the CSI (Customer Service Index) results for each dealership and – if they pass the minimum thresholds – pay out incentives to the best performers (either as a % of sales or £ per car sold)… The best franchisees also make sure that incentives that we put in place 'flow down' to their key personnel (certainly on new sales and CSI scores)…

Bryn Thomas, PSA Citroen (Case Study 6)

[I]t is important that operational transformation is led by leaders with credibility who really 'monitor the incentive to perform' and care about franchisee profit… winning franchisors make 'good' sustainable profit rather than 'bad' short-termist gains! …

Patricia Thomas, Domino's (Case Study 8)

[Dome] is a highly sought after franchise in the Australian market... The turnovers and EBITDA of the new stores are industry leading... Franchisees can generate impressive ROIs on agreements that run on 10–5–5 or 10–10 terms...

Andrew Thomas, Dome Café (Case Study 9)

- *Capital and Growth (Franchisee)*

How do franchisees reciprocate monetarily? In the main, franchisees reciprocate by driving financial performance, investing capital (when required) in new technology/machinery, deploying funds for more stores and being receptive to trialling new initiatives for their own self-interest and the benefit of the wider system – as snapshots of several franchisee case studies show:

[W]e did deliver the plan for growth and **hit the 'numbers'** as expected – we did what we said we would do! – something that was well received by the franchisor... Today, I have four stores...

Richard Johnson, Domino's (Case Study 13)

[S]uccessful franchisees saw themselves as having good numbers skills allied to an obsession with *benchmarking*. Great franchisees (who generate healthy fee income!) tended to be naturally competitive... in fact many were frustrated that they did not get better information on how they were faring against their 'managed store' cousins! ...

Adrian Rhodes, GlobalBrand (Case Study 12)

It is quite notable that many MUFs are granted more units over time once they have proved themselves financially...

Lee Sheldon, MMU (Case Study 15)

[Franchisors] seek out willing franchisees who will trial new revenue-driving growth (or cost saving!) initiatives that might be of financial benefit to all parties... they can influence the thinking of the brand owners for the financial benefit of the entire system...

Andrew Emmerson, Snappies/Dunkin' Donuts (Case Study 17)

II. PRODUCT/GOODS EXCHANGE

Retail franchising is an inter-firm relationship where the principal party (the franchisor) agrees with its agent (the franchisee) that it has an obligation to fund/purchase various products and goods. Aside from the brand set-up (i.e. fit out and associated 'hard' costs), franchisees in the UK are usually tied for proprietorial goods which the franchisor designates as 'must stock products'. Access to the branded product attracts varying financial outlay from the franchisee, whilst prescribed goods are usually 'marked up' by the franchisor as an extra form of revenue stream – how can these fees be justified? The answer – supplied by the case-study narratives – is that franchisors must ensure product/goods conform to *high-quality specifications*. The caveat to this quality is that franchisees must *comply* with the standards/obligations associated with the purchase of these products/goods.

- *Quality (Franchisor)*

  In order effectively to engage, regulate and monitor franchisees, franchisors must ensure that their product is simple to understand (for operating purposes), can incorporate changes with ease (during 'global' upgrades and improvements) and is systemised to such a degree that it can be executed consistently and to a high standard by front-line operatives supervised by the franchisee (for quality purposes). The goods sold to the franchisee must also – if they are tied products – have inimitable characteristics (to prevent accusations that the same goods can be bought cheaper elsewhere) and be perceived by franchisees as being of equal – if not superior – quality to comparatively priced goods in the free market. This need was substantiated by several comments by franchisor respondents in the case studies:

  > [W]e tried to keep to this split by maintaining product cash profit (at the expense of erosions in net margin…) [there was no reduction of quality of ingredients]…
  >
  > Chris Moore, Domino's (Case Study 1)

  > Franchise Agreements that emphasise more of a *relational/ mutual* ('good faith) approach to defined rights (franchisee access to quality products and goods) and obligations (franchisee system compliance)… will be more resilient and successful in the long-term than those that don't…
  >
  > John Pratt, Hamilton Pratt (Case Study 3)

> [I]t has meant that DPG is able to concentrate on product quality and digital innovation whilst its franchisees concentrate on operational execution! ...

> Maurice Abboudi, Domino's (Case Study 4)

> [W]hat the values do is provide a strong compass or code of conduct of the way in which people are expected to act... it sustains a quality product, providing a strong backstop to the policies and procedures already in place... It also means that the YHA continues to be a successful and relevant organisation, in spite of the competitive pressures it faces...

> Jerry Robinson, YHA (Case Study 7)

- ### *Compliance (Franchisee)*

  In return for their access to a highly specified system which offers quality product/goods (the 'know how'), franchisees recognised that they must *comply* in order to preserve consistency and brand uniformity. Successful franchisees (most notably MUFs) conform – keeping to the prescribed standards laid out in the Operations Manual (both amenity and operational execution) and adhering to buying requirements. Of course, conformist behaviours might be driven by the fear of penalties for non-compliance but they are also motivated by beneficial outcomes such as greater flexibility (once confidence has been established) and further store-growth opportunities:

  > [S]uccessful franchisees saw themselves as being disciplined – complying with and executing every single aspect of this famous brand: in the jargon of psychology they had high levels of vigilance skills, relishing and being meticulous about product detail in order to protect the quality and reputation of the brand... Franchisees tended to come from *'conformist'* rather than *'creative/exploratory'* backgrounds...

  > Adrian Rhodes, GlobalBrand (Case Study 12)

  > [I]ndeed, I have worked for and advised (MUF) franchisees that have been told that they 'operate the brand better' than the franchisor! ... *why?* ... obviously wishing to retain (and grow) the contract is a large financial incentive for the successful MUF (who will strictly monitor standards and systems adherence)

but it is also true to say that MUFs have *less distractions or noise* than the franchisor...

Lee Sheldon, MMU (Case Study 15)

[O]ver time, as we grew, we tightened up our official liveries (on the vans, menus, packaging and marketing) and adhered to the product standards and obligations outlined in the Franchise Agreement and Operations Manual... This presented a far more professional image to our franchisor, customers and prospective franchisees... It also gave our franchisor greater faith in our ability to execute the 'basics' well – granting us extra latitude to experiment with the offer...

Alex Dawson, Café2U (Case Study 18)

III. SERVICES EXCHANGE

The third archetype of transactional exchange is services and support. In classic business terms, the 'servitisation' of products – the provision of added-value advice to enhance delivery – is a useful way of generating revenue for owners. In franchising – like product/goods exchange above – services provided by the franchisor must be paid for by the franchisee: hence the necessity for high levels of impactful *expertise*. In return, successful franchisees will *collaborate* actively with support services to enhance their delivery and execution.

- **Expertise (Franchisor)**

  Previous reference (see Chapter 3) has been made to the nature of support services typically offered by retail franchisors. A major theme that resonates throughout the case-study accounts is the vital importance of services being delivered by experienced functional and/or field-based experts who can add significant value to store operations. Franchisees sign up for long periods of time – it is important that franchisors maintain a modicum of stability amongst their management cadre in order to maintain credibility and influence with their franchisees.

  [B]uilding up the network, we were signing up franchisees for long periods of time... it was important (doubly so when we abandoned owned stores) to have knowledgeable, credible leaders... with high levels of operational/support expertise and strong franchisee ties... You have to have a system based on long-term relationships, high levels of operational/support expertise and strong franchisee ties... The fact that at one time our leadership team had an average of 13 years' service was incredibly important for information/knowledge continuity purposes...

Chris Moore, Domino's (Case Study 1)

With regards to support services, they expertly refined two 'hygiene' aspects of the operation well: **robust** *IT platforms* (for BOH ordering/replenishment and FOH sales reporting) and **'top draw'** *Logistics systems* (that focused upon delivering the 'right product, right quality, right time')... They also provided excellent local marketing and training support packages, professional field-based support and a list of recommended suppliers that could provide maintenance, refurbishment, payroll and legal support etc. ...

Paul Daynes, Musgrave (Case Study 5)

To this end we have an extremely 'lean' support centre (only 20 staff with high levels of functional expertise – particularly our food safety consultant)...

Andrew Thomas, Dome Café (Case Study 9)

- **Collaboration (Franchisee)**

  In return, good franchisees will interact with franchisor management in a variety of forums: in store (meetings and pilot initiatives), district meetings, representation on elected regional/national advisory councils, conferences and such like. What the best franchisees do is co-operate and collaborate with centre and field-based personnel to benefit not only themselves (in terms of learning and profile) but also the wider network (in terms of *revenue-enhacing* or *cost-saving ideas* derived from their close proximity to day-to-day operations and local markets/customers).

  [T]o be invited onto these [advisory] groups was a privilege and we expected mature contributions from 'seasoned' people...

  Chris Moore, Domino's (Case Study 1)

[C]ollaborative mindset (essential amongst franchisees) – ... the ability to share ideas with peers/support services and participate in open feedback channels...

Jerry Marwood, Spar (Case Study 11)

[B]ut I have to say that it was a highly collaborative arrangement... communications were exceptionally good with frequent meetings between key Rosinter staff and TGI's senior EMEA International Franchise team members...

Ian Dunstall, Rosinter (Case Study 16)

Collaborative – ... *Dunkin' Donuts* had an excellent system whereby they nominated 'franchisee leaders' – individuals that were influential within their districts and regions – to act as 'go to' people for pilots and tests (such as new operational systems, store designs and product innovation); they did this on the basis that these individuals had a high degree of credibility and if they 'gave the nod', the rest of the network would 'buy in'...

Andrew Emmerson, Snappies/Dunkin' Donuts
(Case Study 17)

RELATIONAL MECHANISMS

As opposed to economically based transactional exchange, relational archetypes of exchange between business partners include behaviourally based forms such as *love*, *status* and *information* (Foa and Foa 1974, 1980). In retail franchising, reciprocation (see Figure 8.2) occurs between parties placed within each archetype, increasing trust-based mutual interdependencies. Indeed, according to Chris Moore (ex-CEO of Domino's, Case Study 1) the influence of 'softer' relational mechanisms between the two parties is far more important than that of transactional ones:

Franchisors will win if they understand that, firstly, it is more about the *EQ (emotional intelligence)* than the IQ (the hard 'number grinding' *financial advantages*)...

This is a view endorsed by John Pratt (Hamilton Pratt, Case Study 3), who sees a trend for franchised contracts becoming 'more relational in nature' with obligations of 'good faith' that cut both ways and Andrew Emmerson (Snappies/Dunkin' Donuts, Case Study 17) who believed that 'softer' informal relational means of influence are often more effective than 'hard' transactional formal methods'.

I. LOVE EXCHANGE

The first archetype of relational business exchange is love. This might sound trite or even overstated. However, its underlying supposition – the formation of deep, trusting and meaningful ties in which both parties stick together through 'thick and thin' – carries a high degree of resonance in the field of franchising. Success in retail franchising is hard won: the work is arduous (involving multiple daily service-based transactions) and the competitive challenges are significant. Both parties must establish incredibly deep bonds in order to overcome (numerous) obstacles in order to achieve successful commercial outcomes. As the case studies demonstrate, one way franchisors achieve this is through deploying effective *recognition* mechanisms. Franchisees, on the other hand, reciprocate through high levels of loyalty and *commitment* to the cause.

- **Recognition (Franchisor)**

  Successful franchisors understand that they must combine function with emotion. That is to say, designing and rolling-out a successful concept is not only dependent upon rational execution (supervising, checking and monitoring) – it's success is also contingent upon generating/sustaining a positive 'hearts and minds' culture. Obviously economic factors have a major part to play in a successful franchising partnership but it is the ability of franchisors to inspire, engage and recognise – creating meaning and sense of 'higher purpose' – which will augment/sustain fruitful relations:

  > [At the Conference] We chanted 'Who Are We: Domino's!, What Are We: Number One!, What Do We Do? – Sell More Pizzas, Have More Fun!!!' ... This 'anglicised Americanism', as I call it, might seem trite to cynics – but it worked...
  >
  > Chris Moore, Domino's (Case Study 1)

[T]hey encouraged all stakeholders (franchisees, customers and suppliers) to attach and engage with the brand by having a *'local' focus*; insisting that franchisees placed their name on the brand fascias (e.g. Warners's Budgens) [enhancing local recognition] of the owner/proprietor…

Paul Daynes, Musgrave (Case Study 5)

Our annual 'Citroen Award for Excellence' is in an incredible motivator…

Bryn Thomas, PSA Citroen (Case Study 6)

I started to work on our relationships with our franchisees by having informal meals and drinks with many of them, 'bringing them back into balance' (overcoming objections and problem raising) by recognising their contribution… asking about *how* they had got here today – listening to their stories, which almost served as a conscious reminder to them *why* what they were doing was important…

Patricia Thomas, Domino's (Case Study 8)

• Commitment (Franchisee)

How do franchisees reciprocate? It is an empirical observation that franchisees transition through a life-cycle curve of attitudinal disposition towards their franchisor (see Chapter 5), going through phases of initial commitment/dependency, disillusionment, challenge and then (grudging) acceptance. The best maintain a sense of perspective throughout – taking a view that ultimately the brand is 'bigger' than themselves! Those that sustain buy-in, belief, loyalty, energy and effort are more likely to prosper than those that are 'shirkers' and 'free riders' – work shy, negative, disruptive and parasitical. Those with the right mindset can be described as 'emotionally contagious' – positively influencing the attitudes and behaviours of both their staff, peers and (sometimes) franchisor management.

[Winning franchisees have] passion, energy, belief and commitment to the cause… energising those around you to demonstrate the same behaviours! …

Chris Moore, Domino's (Case Study 1)

[Franchisee key attributes include] *conviction* – … the ability to trial, test and see things through… to keep going when others might give up or question 'why'! … 'members' who get what we are trying to do and are in it for the long term… *competitiveness* – … to enjoy being the best… wanting to win awards and receive industry/peer recognition… a burning desire to be the best…

> Jerry Marwood, Spar (Case Study 11)

[Great franchisees have] utter commitment to, and belief in, the brand. What did this mean? Successful franchisees willingly bought into all aspects of the brand, namely: its identity, values, service delivery system and massive commitment to training: above all they bought 'the system'… Great franchisees had the emotional intelligence and energy to manage effectively a wide range of people… They were astute in the hiring decisions – taking on 'cheerful staff' who gave great customer service in spite of some of the repetitive, messy jobs they were called on to do… 'enriching' mundane jobs through providing excellent training and progression opportunities… and they didn't just claim to have motivated staff: *research again confirmed it…*

> Adrian Rhodes, GlobalBrand (Case Study 12)

Make no mistake, running a franchise is really hard work – you really have to put in the hours to be successful…

> Richard Johnson, Domino's (Case Study 13)

I have known franchisees that have 'loved' their brand and experimented… committed to make things better! … not asking permission but seeking forgiveness afterwards! …

> Andrew Emmerson, Snappies/Dunkin' Donuts
> (Case Study 17)

II. STATUS EXCHANGE

The second form of relational archetype in business exchange is *status*. Commonly, status is viewed as a transactional exchange device, implying patronage, preferment and reward. Status within this context, however, means business members' perception of their own and others' position within the hierarchy and their ability to influence events. In 'managed' contexts, status within organisations is clearly delineated through distinctive command structures, grading systems and job titles. How does hierarchy manifest itself in franchising? Previous studies have shown that franchisors operating an 'executive leadership' approach in franchising might be more effective than those deploying a 'participative leadership' style for reasons of speed, decisiveness and impact. Indeed, one senior franchisor respondent commented that he believed the best approach was to behave like a 'benevolent dictator' (although he caveated this statement by saying that he never took major decisions without 'picking the phone up' to judge the reaction of his most influential MUFs in the system!)

It follows, then, that in retail franchising some franchisors might believe that – due to contractual arrangements – they can adopt a 'master–servant' approach with their franchisees. They are mistaken! Any abuse of their perceived power resources – derived from their senior position in the contractual arrangements – will lead to discord and disunity (and possibly mutiny). Indeed – as the case studies in this book show – franchisors who adopt an 'executive leadership' approach within franchising do not exclude discussion and *inclusivity* – they merely reserve the right to make the final decision. In addition, where they act inclusively, they expect franchisees to act maturely and *respectfully* in return.

- **Inclusivity (Franchisor)**

  Throughout the research, franchisors stressed the importance of listening and adopting a 'sell' rather than 'tell' approach with their franchisees. This is not to say that they advocated handing over decision-making processes – rather they sought to set up structures and mechanisms through which franchisees had some influence on important decisions. This would turn the rhetoric that their franchisees were 'partners' into some semblance of reality. Additionally, franchisors operating lean support structures and – in some instances – no managed estate, recognised that they needed to co-opt the views and opinions of franchisees for sound commercial reasons. Evidence of inclusive behaviour in the case studies included:

  > [We sought to] produce a culture that was *'akin to a club'*... we held two major set-piece events which were *deliberately inclusive*... we didn't only invite franchisees, we also invited their partners... and franchisees invited managers, along with other staff members and drivers... for a few days we were all

together… with precious little sense of hierarchy and looking forward to winning together over the next year! …

Chris Moore, Domino's (Case Study 1)

[To produced good franchise contracts,] rather than describing duties, responsibilities and obligations in terms of 'you'… talk in terms of 'we'… for instance 12-month non-compete clauses can be drafted with the opener 'we agree that' rather than 'you will not'! …

John Pratt, Hamilton Pratt (Case Study 3)

[One of our core values is] *inclusivity*… the CEO and her senior leadership team are extremely 'non-hierarchical' and visible within the business, regularly visiting hostels and communicating directly with managers/franchisees (business briefings, award ceremonies, family events etc.)… also (crucially in my view) *their decision-making* constantly reinforces the value set of the organisation (particularly around sustainability, inclusivity and trust) to an extent I have not previously witnessed in corporates! …

Jerry Robinson, YHA (Case Study 7)

- **Franchisee Respect**

  Such an inclusive approach is something to be welcomed and embraced by franchisees. Unfortunately, due to petty disputes, minor grievances and immature behaviour, some franchisees might abuse this approach. Successful franchisees, however, will reciprocate through *respectful* attitudes and behaviours: showing manners/maturity in meetings, keeping disputes 'in house' and actively appreciating the contribution of others (franchisor staff and peers).

  [A]ll were treated respectfully as equal partners at these meetings: all views were counselled… The best franchisees who commented on 'contentious' issues such as the supply chain or cost of goods did so politely and *rationally*… DPG was really a club – and to be a member of that club, all participants (both franchisor and franchisee) had to abide by certain rules so that both sides could win through 'selling more pizzas, having more fun! …

  Chris Moore, Domino's (Case Study 1)

[T]he guild system (arranged on district, regional and national levels) is an extremely collaborative and co-operative arrangement built around respectful relations... we pride ourselves on encouraging 'peer-to-peer' idea sharing OR 'crowd sourcing' for ideas... The best seem able to 'jog and chew gum' – they know it is not an 'either/or' choice – success rests on making mature choices at the right time, in the best interests of the wider organisation and consumer! ...

Jerry Marwood, Spar (Case Study 11)

[A]lthough it is important that the partnership is an economic success, this in itself will be an outcome of close 'trust-based' partnership working... This is built up through close collaboration: each side delivering on its promises... listening/respecting the contribution of one another...

Lee Sheldon, MMU (Case Study 15)

'Grown up' franchisees can also affect policy through forming deep bonds with franchisor personnel... getting to know one another well – understanding hopes/desires/fears – leads to greater trust and mutual respect...

Andrew Emmerson, Snappies/Dunkin' Donuts
(Case Study 17)

III. INFORMATION EXCHANGE

The third form of relational exchange in business is information. Its success as an exchange mechanism is shaped by two dimensions: process and content. Effective information/communication *processes* are characteristically frequent and accessible (web technology being a formidable enabler in current times), its *content* dependable, accurate and truthful. Why is this important in retail franchising? First, there is the problem of multi-site distance where franchisees situated a long way from the centre – receiving intermittent visits from company personnel – can feel physically detached and isolated. Second, the onset of web technology over the past twenty years has made access to information far easier, meaning that at times organisations can be behind other sources in relaying information to their members. Franchisors therefore require information dissemination mechanisms that are quick and – most importantly – transparent and *honest*.

Reciprocating in this spirit of openness, franchisees must be prepared to *share* information with their franchisor, peers and staff.

- **Honesty (Franchisor)**

  Whether they were being disingenuous or not, most respondents during the research agreed that franchisors should attempt to communicate authentically, transparently and honestly with their franchisees. Sharing information that has a high degree of commercial sensitivity – such as 'tied product' margins – might seem risky, in that it might contaminate relations between the two parties if the franchisor is perceived to be 'gorging' at the franchisee's expense. However, it is better that the franchisor discloses all available information (performance, margins, fee structures etc.) openly for franchisees to challenge rather than leaving them to find out the 'truth' through other sources. Trust can only built and sustained if franchisors are honest with their franchisees, something that was surfaced time and again in the case studies.

  > [M]aking statements [in the Franchise Agreement] such as 'we shall always endeavour to communicate openly and honestly' will not only reinforce the relational rhetoric in the sales brochures but will also create a more conducive 'going in' mentality... In terms of the Operating Manual – as I said – it is certainly helpful if the franchisor knows it is part of his job description... and certainly his operations/support teams' role to update it! ... this will only improve relations: franchisees like to know what they've got do and how they can do it more effectively...
  >
  > John Pratt, Hamilton Pratt (Case Study 3)

  > In Citroen UK, we have honest and accurate real-time 'output' and 'input' data/information systems in place to ensure that the sales and aftersales performance of our franchised network (SUF and MUF) is properly monitored and 'animated'... control systems work when they are transparent and fair...
  >
  > Bryn Thomas, PSA Citroen (Case Study 6)

  > We also set up regular calendar communications events which were designed to inform franchisees honestly and directly what we were doing, seeking their buy-in to changes... I used my

experiences in the US as a powerful anecdote to highlight how operations that lose focus on product quality and speed of delivery can 'drift off'... but what I also did was to demonstrate empirically a financial link between investing in staff training, deployment and equipment, their positive effects upon operational execution and customer satisfaction/sales out-turns...

Patricia Thomas, Domino's (Case Study 8)

[W]e are believers in communicating honestly with our franchisees; setting unwaveringly high standards and expectations that our franchisees both understand and buy into...

Andrew Thomas, Dome Café (Case Study 9)

- **Sharing (Franchisee)**

Franchisees are not only passive recipients of information, they are active conduits in the process of *sharing* information with their immediate stakeholders. With regards to the franchisor, successful franchisees will disclose sensitive financial information, whether or not obligated to do so, either for the purposes of 'performance improvement' discussions or to mitigate the impact of any 'nasty surprises'. Within their own businesses, successful franchisees will generally share information with their managers/staff, imitating their owner's frankness and honesty. Finally, franchisees will share information (insights and knowledge) with peers, expecting reciprocal intelligence in return. No franchisee can be an 'island unto himself' – sharing information is critical for improvement purposes:

[G]reat local knowledge enabled franchisees to win on the ground and (when shared) benefit the wider system...

Chris Moore, Domino's (Case Study 1)

[O]ur franchisees and their managers/staff... share ideas over the interactive on-line platform Yammer... this has proved particularly useful for 'idea swapping' around growing top-line sales at key seasonal events (Mother's Day this year was one of the biggest trading days in our history), community initiatives, events and evening time-slot 'filling' ('show-and-tell' events, jazz sessions etc.)...

Andrew Thomas, Dome Café (Case Study 9)

[W]e pride ourselves on encouraging 'peer-to-peer' idea sharing OR 'crowd sourcing' for ideas...

Jerry Marwood, Spar (Case Study 11)

[A]s we grew, we needed to communicate more effectively with our franchisor and franchisees in order to keep both parties onboard... Interaction with our franchisor became more frequent as we became more successful – sharing vital information with them to retain good relations was essential... as the network grew... we got clusters of franchisees together to share their ideas with both us and one another – a two-hour meeting was always followed by a meal where people could relax and 'bond'...

Alex Dawson, Café2U (Case Study 18)

SUMMARY

This concluding chapter has attempted to bring the main strands of the book together, principally drawing upon the empirical evidence from the case studies to propose a new **Franchise Exchange Model (FEM)**. This is important. To date, scholars have defined narrowly (either in transactional or relational terms) what constitutes success in a franchising context. Practitioners have written books that have described 'how to' set up a franchise and what franchisees should look out for when purchasing one. This book has taken a dual approach, *first*, structuring itself around the sequence of activities franchisors (design, deliver and develop) and franchisees (engage, execute and evolve) should undertake to make a success of franchising. *Second*, the chapter summaries and this conclusion have – by drawing on the powerful set of case studies – provided an elevated degree of analysis that might provide universal explanations as to how both sides can win in franchising. *'The desired end'* in retail franchising is a high level of *mutual interdependence* between two parties. This mutuality, however, will only be generated/sustained by *'the means'* – both parties abiding by certain rules of *exchange*. As the **FEM** highlights in Figure 8.2, franchise parties that reciprocate around the main transactional (money, product/goods and services) and relational (love, status and information) archetypes of business exchange are more likely to be successful than those that don't. Put simply, success in retail franchising comes through a pre-disposition to 'give and take' rather than 'take and take'.

Alon, I. 2006. 'Market Conditions Favoring Master International Franchising'. *Multinational Business Review*. 14 (2), 67–82.

Anwar, S. 2011. 'Franchising: category issues, changing dynamics and competitiveness'. *International Journal of Commerce and Management*. 21 (3), 241–55.

ATKearney. 2012. *Global Retail Expansion: Keeps on Moving*. ATKearney Inc.

Baena, V. 2012. 'Market conditions driving international franchising in emerging markets'. *International Journal of Emerging Markets*. 7 (1), 49–71.

Blau, P.M. 1964. *Exchange and Power in Social Life*. London: Wiley.

Bradach, J. 1995. 'Chains within chains: The role of multi-unit franchisees'. *Journal of Marketing Channels*. 4 (1/2), 65–81.

Castrogiovanni, G., and Justis, R. 1998. 'Franchising configurations and transactions'. *Journal of Consumer Marketing*. 15 (2), 170–90.

Charity, P. 2014a. 'Papa John's franchisee plans five sites thanks to incentives'. PropelInfo (28 January), 1.

Charity, P. 2014b. 'Marston's boosts online communication for franchisees'. PropelInfo (29 January), 1.

Cohen, A.R., and Bradford, D.L. 1989. *Influence without Authority*. USA: Wiley.

Combs, J., and Ketchen, D. 1999. 'Can Capital Scarcity Help Agency Theory Explain Franchising? A Test of the Capital Scarcity Hypothesis'. *Academy of Management Journal*. 42 (2), 196–207.

Cropanzano, R., and Mitchell, M.S. 2005. 'Social exchange theory: an interdisciplinary review'. *Journal of Management*. 31, 874–900.

Dant, R., Weaven, S., and Baker, B. 2013. 'Influence of personality traits on perceived relationship quality within a franchisee–franchisor context'. *European Journal of Marketing*. 47 (1/2), 279–302.

Diaz-Bernardo, R. 2013. Managing a Franchise System: A Literature Review and a Synthesis. *Journal of Business and Economics Research*. 11 (7), 293–96.

DiPietro, R., Severt, D., Welsh, D., and Raven, P. 2008. 'Franchisee leadership traits vs. manager leadership traits: An exploratory study comparing hope, leadership, commitment and service delivery'. *International Entrepreneurship and Management Journal*. 4 (1), 63–78.

Doherty, A. 2007. 'The internationalization of retailing: factors influencing the choice of franchising as a market entry strategy'. *International Journal of Service Industry Management*. 18 (2), 184–205.

Duckett, B., and Monaghan, P. 2007. *How to Franchise Your Business*. Oxford: How To Books.

Edger, 2014. *Professional Area Management – Leading at a Distance in Multi-Unit Operations*. Oxford: Libri.

Edger, 2013. *International Multi-Unit Leadership – Developing Local Leaders in International Multi-Site Operations*. Farnham: Gower.

Edger, 2012. *Effective Multi-Unit Leadership – Local Leadership in Multi-Site Situations*. Farnham: Gower.

Eisenhardt, K. 1989. 'Agency Theory: An Assessment and Review'. *Academy of Management Review*. 14 (1), 57–74.

Emerson, R.M. 1976. 'Social exchange theory'. *Annual Review of Sociology*. 2, 335–62.

Foa, U., and Foa, E. 1980. Resource theory: Interpersonal behavior as exchange, in K. Gergen, M. Greenberg and R. Willis (eds), *Social exchange: Advances in theory and research*. NY: Plenum.

Foa, U., and Foa, E. 1974. *Societal structures of the mind*. Springfield IL: Charles C Thomas.

Garg, V. 2013. 'Does Multi-unit Franchising Aid Differentiation? An Exposition'. *Journal of Applied Management and Entrepreneurship*. 18 (1), 3–26.

Gassenheimer, J., Baucus, D., and Baucus, M. 1996. 'Cooperative Arrangements among Entrepreneurs: An Analysis of Opportunism and Communication in Franchise Structures'. *Journal of Business Research*. 36, 67–79.

Gellhorn, E. 1967. 'Limitations on Contract Termination Rights – Franchise Cancellations'. *Duke Law Journal*. 3, 465–501.

Gibson, C. 2010. *Franchising Exposed*. London: alliebooks.

Gouldner, A. 1960. 'The Norm of Reciprocity: A Preliminary Statement'. *American Sociological Review*. 25, 1–16.

Grace, D., Weaven, S., Frazer, L., and Giddings, J. 2013. 'Examining the Role of Franchisee Normative Expectations in Relationship Evaluation'. *Journal of Retailing*. 89 (2), 219–30.

Harmon, T., and Griffiths, M. (2008) 'Franchisee Perceived Relationship Value'. *Journal of Business & Industrial Marketing*. 23:4.

Hofstede, G. 1991. *Cultures and Organisations*. London: McGraw Hill.

Hollander, R. 2005. 'From Single Operators to Multi-Unit Owners: Helping Franchisees Make the Leap'. *Franchising World*. 37 (5), 51–4.

Hunt, S., and Nevin, J. 1974. 'Power in a channel of distribution: Sources and consequences'. *Journal of Marketing Research*. 11, 186–93.

Hussain, D., and Windsperger, J. 2011. 'Multi-Unit Franchising: A Comparative Case Analysis'. *Journal of Applied Business Research*. 27 (1), 103–11.

Jensen, M., and Meckling, W. 1976. 'Theory of the Firm: Managerial Behaviour, Agency Costs and Ownership Structure'. *Journal of Financial Economics*. 3, 305–60.

Kalnins, A. 2004. 'An Empirical Analysis of Territorial Encroachment Within Franchised and Company-Owned Branded Chains'. *Marketing Science*. 23 (4), 476–89.

Kaufmann, P., and Dant, R. 1992. 'The dimensions of commercial exchange'. *Marketing Letters*. 3 (2), 171–85.

Klein, B. 1995. 'The Economics of Franchise Contracts'. *Journal of Corporate Finance*. 2, 9–37.

Kroc, R. 1997/1977. *Grinding It Out*. Chicago IL: St Martin's.

Lafontaine, F. 1992. 'Agency Theory and Franchising: Some Empirical Results'. *Rand Journal of Economics*, 23 (2), 263–83.

Lawrence, B., and Kaufmann, P. 2011. 'Identity in Franchise Systems: The Role of Franchisee Associations'. *Journal of Retailing*. 87 (3), 285–305.

Madhok, A., and Tallman, S. 1998. 'Resources transactions and rents: Managing value through inter-firm collaborative relationships'. *Organization Science*. 9 (3), 326–39.

Meeker, B.F. 1971. Decisions and exchange. *American Sociological Review*. 36: 485–95.

Mendelsohn, M. 1999. *Franchising*. Cassell: London.

Michael, S., and Combs, J. 2008. 'Entrepreneurial Failure: The Case of Franchisees'. *Journal of Small Business Management*. 46 (1), 73–90.

Morrison, K. 1997. 'How Franchisee Job Satisfaction Affects Performance, Organizational Commitment, Franchisor Relations, and Intention to Remain'. *Journal of Small Business*. 35 (3), 39–67.

NatWest/BFA. 2013. *Nat West and British Franchising Association Franchise Survey*. London: NatWest.

Palamountain, J. 1955. *The Politics of Distribution*. Cambridge MA: Harvard University Press.

Parsa, H. 1996. 'Franchisor–Franchisee relationships in quick-service restaurant systems'. *Cornell Hotel and Restaurant Administration Quarterly*. 37 (3), 42–50.

Pfister, E., Deffains, B., Doriat-Duban, M., and Saussier, S. 2006. 'Institutions and Contracts: Franchising'. *European Journal of Law and Economics*. 21, 53–78.

Rubin, P. 1978. 'The Theory of the Firm and the Structure of the Franchise Contract'. *Journal of Law and Economics*. 21, 223–33.

Saks, A.M. 2006. 'Antecedents and Consequences of Employee Engagement'. *Journal of Managerial Psychology*. 21 (7), 600–12.

Schul, P., Pride, W., and Little, T. 1983. 'The impact of channel leadership behaviour on interchannel conflict'. *Journal of Marketing*. 47, 21–34.

Shane, S. 1996. 'Why Franchise Companies Expand Overseas'. *Journal of Business Venturing*. 11, 73–88.

Sorenson, O., and Sorenson, J. 2001. 'Finding the Right Mix: Organisational Learning and Chain Performance'. *Strategic Management Journal*. 22, 713–24.

Spinelli, S., and Birley, S. 1998. An empirical evaluation of conflict in the franchise system. *British Journal of Management*. 9, 301–24.

Spinelli, S., Rosenburg, R., and Birley, S. 2004. *Franchising: Pathway to Wealth Creation*. New Jersey: Prentice Hall.

Strutton, D., Pelton, L., and Lumpkin, J. 1995. 'Psychological climate in franchising system channels and franchisor–franchisee solidarity'. *Journal of Business Research*. 34, 81–91.

Weaven, S., and Frazer, L. 2007a. 'Expansion through multi-unit franchising – Australian franchisors reveal their motivations'. *International Small Business Journal*. 19 (7), 173–205.

Weaven, S., and Frazer, L. 2007b. 'Mature franchise systems use multiple unit franchising to leverage learning economies and sustain systemwide growth'. *Asia Pacific Journal of Marketing and Logistics*. 19 (2), 107–26.

INDEX